Miracle of *Belief*

The Story of a
Six-Year-Old
Heart Hero

Caleb~ Possible
Anything is Possible!
You are a true Hero!
Sondra Dubas

Ashley
Dubas!!
♡♡

Miracle of Belief

The Story of a Six-Year-Old Heart Hero

Sondra Dubas

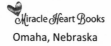
Miracle Heart Books
Omaha, Nebraska

ISBN: 978-0-9892172-1-7 (paperback)
        978-0-9892172-2-4 (kindle)
        978-0-9892172-3-1 (ePub)

LCCN: 2013936657
Library of Congress Cataloging information on file with publisher.

Design and production: Concierge Marketing, Inc.
Printed in the United States.

10   9   8   7   6   5   4

*To my beautiful daughters
who are my world and to my husband
for supporting me in life and my work
and for understanding why I needed to tell our story*

Contents

Preface. 1
Introduction. 3

Part I   When the Unexpected Happens. 5
    1   Preparing for Impact 7
    2   The Unexpected 17
    3   Breakdown 33
    4   Waking Up. 65

Part II   Learning Everything All Over Again. 103
    5   The Road to Rehabilitation 105
    6   Regaining Independence. 115
    7   Hearing Her Voice Again 131
    8   I Can Stand on My Own Two Feet. 143
    9   I Can Walk on My Own Two Feet 155
   10   I Can See with My Own Two Eyes. 167
   11   Home Sweet Home. 177

Part III   Getting Back to Living. 183
   12   Day Rehab. 185
   13   New Normal 201
   14   What It's Like to Be a Heart Hero 211
   15   Choices 217
   16   Letting Go 221

Ashley Today 227
About Heart Heroes, Inc. 229
Special Tributes 233
About the Author 237

Preface

The moment we learned that Ashley experienced significant complications during her heart surgery, our optimism and hope for a smooth, routine operation were dealt a crushing blow. And momentarily, life as we knew it stopped. I had wished for a book like this to be given to me to tell me what to do. I wanted an instruction book for coping. Since I didn't find that one existed, we figured out on our own what worked for us.

My primary goal with sharing our story is so that our experience can help others to cope with unexpected tragedies, especially those involving their children. We also learned many valuable life lessons from the experience, which are also shared throughout the book. For me, and for our family, we viewed it as "an awakening."

I have always enjoyed inspirational quotes and relevant bible passages. There were many times during our journey that a particular bible verse or quote would pop out at me from a book or even a billboard. Or someone would send me a message with a quote that was just what I needed to get me through the day. I've included many of my favorites throughout the book.

I want to make one thing very clear. My husband and I have never felt the need to place blame for any of the events that happened to our daughter. We believe everything happens for a reason and that some things can't be explained. Our daughter recovered. And our lives were forever changed. This book is written as a positive tool to help others find strategies for coping.

Written permission has been granted for all names used in the writing of this book. Other names have been changed or concealed to protect the privacy of those individuals.

Much of this book has been based on the actual daily online journal that I wrote during the days that this occurred. Those journal entries have been preserved in their original context with minor modifications.

Introduction

How could the journey of Ashley, our six-year-old little girl, from unexpected brain injury through recovery inspire thousands of people from coast to coast? Hundreds of people followed her story by way of Internet technology day-by-day, tens of thousands of times in total. People offered thousands of messages of encouragement and support for us along the way.

I have marveled at why so many people are drawn to the story of our little girl—one young life hanging in the balance. What is it that people are searching for? Is it the lack of meaning, purpose, or direction that so many people feel in their lives? Are we all waiting for the "life-changing" event that will inspire us to change our course in life? What if that event never comes? Is surviving each day good enough? Or can we all find the power within us to live the life we choose? What happens when we funnel this kind of belief into our daily lives?

How can something so traumatic be a blessing? A gift? What do we really know about the power of our minds? As witness to the healing power of the brain, from the outside, there are still many mysteries. Perhaps this story can only enhance our belief in the power of simply believing that anything is possible.

It is our hope that through this account of our daughter's tragic brain injury and amazing recovery we can capture the essence of why this event changed our lives. And why it impacted the lives of so many other people. Perhaps yours.

Many people offered encouragement over the past four years about the idea of sharing our story. I've carried that notion in my head all along and have always thought "someday, we'll tell the story." I think we needed some time to get back to normal life and, of course, make some drastic changes in our lives and adjust accordingly. God continued to provide the "signs" that this book should be published.

Recently, a friend of a friend made a significant impression on me when he looked me in the eyes and very boldly asked, "Who are you depriving of hearing this amazing story that could benefit from hearing it?"

I felt this was God's work in nudging me to do His calling. I have always believed that God put these experiences in our lives to learn from them and inspire others to make transformations in their faith and in their lives.

"I tell you the truth, unless you change and become like little children, you will never enter the kingdom of heaven."

— Jesus of Nazareth

part one

When the
Unexpected Happens

> "What we have once enjoyed, we can never lose. All that we love becomes a part of us.
> — Helen Keller

> "Live it. Experience it. Cherish it. Because you never know if you'll get it back.
> — Sondra Dubas

"" **Children reinvent your world for you.** **""**

— Susan Sarandon

Chapter One

Preparing for Impact

From the moment Ashley was born we began asking the question, "Why?" Why was our child born with a heart defect? Why did we have to deal with this? Why did this happen and what went wrong? It was a healthy pregnancy! Most importantly—WHY DID GOD LET THIS HAPPEN?

And then we fell in love with this sweet little girl and it didn't matter what we had to endure or why, we knew we were chosen to be her parents for some very special reason. And so our journey began. Ashley had her first open-heart surgery at the age of three months in September 2001. She was a tiny little baby, and it was impossible to imagine that a person so small could endure such a major operation. It was not easy.

She had breathing complications after surgery and had to have a tracheotomy, a tube inserted into the neck, to assist the airway in breathing. She spent two and a half months in the hospital, followed by in-home nursing care for the next year and a half. My husband, Tim, and I had been married ten years prior to her birth. Quite frankly, we were nervous about changing diapers! We were not at all prepared to take care of such a "high-tech" baby.

Ashley went on to have a heart catheterization, other surgeries to remove the tracheotomy tube, repair the hole in her neck, and regular visits with cardiologists and pulmonologists. There was absolutely nothing "normal" about our life. Yet somehow we managed through it all. We continued on with our careers and jobs. Eventually life got easier. We were delighted to be blessed with another sweet baby girl four years later and grateful that Nicole was born "heart healthy."

Even though life was moving along in normal fashion, there was always that looming feeling of knowing that Ashley would need to return again multiple times for heart surgery throughout her life. She was born with a hole in her heart and no pulmonary valve and, therefore, had an implanted valve that kept her heart pumping blood to her lungs.

The advances in modern pediatric cardiology have made it possible for children like Ashley to survive and live normal, healthy lives. However, an implanted valve does not grow as the body grows. And Ashley would eventually outgrow the valve and require a replacement.

And so this is where this story begins. Ashley was a bright, happy six-year-old when the time had arrived for her to have surgery to replace her heart valve. We had been planning the date for the previous six months and preparing ourselves for this event.

For me, it felt kind of like being nine months pregnant with your first baby and scared of what's about to happen, but knowing there's absolutely no turning back! There was no choice. Ashley needed this surgery in order to continue to grow and thrive. We knew that we must accept that. However, we were scared based on what had happened with Ashley's first surgery and the breathing difficulties. At this point her lungs had matured, so that was not a concern. It was just the fear of the unknown. It was the fear of all the "what-ifs." What if something went wrong? What if the surgery didn't work? And the most horrific thought that we didn't talk about—but that we knew was in the back of our minds—what if she doesn't make it through the surgery?

It is every parent's absolute nightmare. Whether it's a simple procedure of getting the tonsils removed or something as major as this, the fear is there.

The doctors had assured us that this was to be a "routine procedure" as far as open-heart valve replacement surgeries go. She would be in and out of the hospital within five to seven days. So we had set our minds to knowing that we would just need to be strong and get through the next week, and then we'd be right back to normal life again. We would put our faith and trust in the Lord that this would, in fact, be the simple, routine procedure that these doctors conducted all the time.

Yet, there were still those moments when I would think, *What if this is the last time...*? I became more aware of the blessings I had with my children every single day and this ominous feeling that things were about to change. About a week before surgery, I panicked when I realized that we didn't have a proper family picture of our entire family! Nicole was only three years old at the time. Although we had pictures taken each year of the girls, we hadn't gotten a family picture taken together.

I made some phone calls and found a photographer. There was no time to buy new clothes for picture-taking, so I pulled together some simple outfits and we went out to a beautiful park for family pictures the weekend prior to surgery. It was the perfect spring day.

That same day was Ashley's dance recital. We went to the salon and had her hair and makeup done, and I doted on her all day just cherishing every moment. I remember sitting in the audience watching her on stage, tears running down my face. I wanted to enjoy the moment in every way, but I also couldn't ignore the lingering thoughts about what the next week had in store for us. I just wanted to dream about my two little sweet girls and all the future dance recitals and happy family times ahead of us.

Preparing Ashley for the surgery was different than the first surgery when she was a baby. At that time, she wasn't yet able to understand what was going on or talk to us about it. She was just

*Our family photo was taken a week
before surgery in a beautiful park.*

a baby. However, a six-year-old knows what's going on and asks a *lot* of questions! For a child who had been through a lot already, this was going to be no walk in the park. Therefore, not only were we coping with our own fears and emotions, we also had to help a child understand what was about to happen to her.

We talked openly with her and we called it her "Big Heart Day"! Ashley and I created an online journal. This would be an online message board so that our friends and family could stay in touch while we went on this next "adventure." We encouraged people to post messages on the message board for Ashley to read.

I had planned to take my laptop with me to the hospital so I could provide updates on her progress via the online journal. I had promised Ashley that I would read all the messages to her. And I thought she would enjoy that while we were searching for ways to pass time until she could heal enough to be released to come home. I was anticipating that one of the biggest challenges was going to be trying to keep an active six-year-old child calm in a hospital bed for multiple days.

We had taken Ashley to "Operation Learn," a pre-op tour at the pediatric hospital for the kids to get a preview of what to expect. We felt that this would help her get comfortable being at the hospital and give her a chance to ask questions of the medical staff who were experienced in dealing with kids having surgery. Ashley acted like a "pro" answering all the nurses' questions about what was going to be taking place. And she asked a lot of good questions: "Am I going to get pokes?" "Will it hurt?" "Will they use the tight blue rubber band on my arm?" "Do I have to wear the hospital pajamas?" I was so proud of her.

Ashley was surprisingly and amazingly brave and talking openly about her surgery. The scariest part for her was knowing that she would have to stay at the hospital for five to seven days. Of course, we continued to remind her that we would be there with her every single moment. We would not leave her alone.

Ashley helped write a little note to tell her story and a little bit about her!

June 12, 2008
10:10 a.m.

About me

My name is Ashley Dubas. I am 6 years old. I have a little sister named Nicole and she thinks I am really cool. I have a dog named Benny, we sometimes call him The Beast! He's a good dog. I like dancing and singing to Hannah Montana and High School Musical. My favorite foods are ice cream, macaroni & cheese, and tacos. I love going to the beach for vacation, and hiking in the mountains.

My mom and dad tell me that I was born with a very special heart. It is called "absent pulmonary valve syndrome" or APVS. When I was a little baby, only 3 months old, the doctor did an operation on my heart and fixed it with a new valve. In May, 2006, I also had a procedure where the doctors put in what is called a stent. On June 19th, 2008, I am having surgery on my heart again to give me a new valve.

Love, Ashley

A week before the scheduled surgery, we met with Ashley's heart surgeon. He had performed her first heart repair in September 2001 when she was three months old. To me, he was like God because he had given us six years of life with our beautiful daughter. You only see the heart surgeon when it's "that time." But he always remembered who we were and asked about Ashley whenever he saw us at fundraisers for congenital heart defects. I had complete faith and confidence in his ability to lead Ashley successfully through this operation and once again restore her heart to its full-functioning ability.

Optimistically this heart surgery would grant her another ten years of life before outgrowing the valve. Ashley was a bright, beautiful, thriving little girl, and we wanted to have complete faith and confidence that her valve replacement surgery would be a success. In reality, we were scared. Looking back I realize that there were many signs beforehand revealing to me that somehow we knew that this event was going to forever change us.

The day before the scheduled surgery was exhausting. We spent the majority of the day at the hospital having pre-op tests run. And if everything looked

Ashley was so happy and proud the day of her dance recital. This is the costume she wore in her performance of "Gee Whiz, I'm in Showbiz."

good, Ashley would have surgery the next day. We just needed to stay positive and "healthy!" It was three hours of visiting with doctors, getting a chest x-ray, having a heart echocardiogram, multiple blood tests, and lots of paperwork explaining the risks of the surgery. The blood draw was quite traumatic—a signal to us that we have some rough days ahead.

Ashley was very brave and cheery ... joking with everyone! We were very amazed at her maturity and positive spirit in dealing with the whole process. I knew in my heart that she had the strength and the willpower to make it through this. The rest we would have to entrust to God and the wonderful talents of her doctors.

At the end of the day, we got the green light to proceed with the scheduled surgery the following day. We were scheduled to arrive at 5:30 a.m., for a 7 a.m. start. She would be anesthetized before any of the "pokes" for IVs would begin. This was something we worked out with the medical team after the traumatic blood draw experience the day before. That would make it easier on her, and on us.

The full procedure was expected to last five to six hours. A lot of time prepping and getting her on the bypass machine and then time after to wrap everything up. The actual heart repair was expected to be about an hour.

All the arrangements had been made. Tim and I had both scheduled time off from work. For me that was something I had negotiated months prior, as I had just started a brand new job. We would have family by our side. Friends were going to help out with Nicole. Overnight bags were packed for Ashley and for me.

We were about to take the biggest leap of faith of our lives. On the eve of Ashley's "Big Heart Day," she remained very strong and her spirits were very high. That night as I tucked our little girls into bed, I remember thinking, *There is a reason God brought her to us ... she is an amazing, special little girl and He must have great things planned for her.*

Life Lesson: You Are Not in Control

As much as we want to believe that we are in control of our destiny in life, this experience taught me that we really are not. Some things we just can't control or understand. You might look at a situation and think, "Life is not fair." And, in fact, many times we asked ourselves, "Why is this happening?"

Then we realized that there must be a greater plan. This had to be part of a bigger picture of what our lives and our daughters' lives were supposed to be. Our acceptance that we are not in control of everything all the time made coping with the situation a lot easier.

Coping Strategies: Embrace All Your Emotions

I remember some very dark moments where my emotions encompassed fear, guilt, remorse, anger, sadness, and even panic. I realized that the more I ignored those emotions, the more they built up inside and eventually created an explosion! The key is to acknowledge them and accept them. They are natural, and they are emotions that anyone in your situation would experience. It is totally normal. Don't be ashamed or guilty. Just embrace them. And then focus on how to shift the emotions that aren't serving you.

"At the bottom of every one of your fears is simply the fear that you can't handle whatever life may bring you. The truth is: If you knew you could handle anything that came your way, what would you possibly have to fear? All you have to do to diminish your fear is to develop more trust in your ability to handle whatever comes your way!"

—*Feel the Fear, And Do It Anyway,*
a book by Susan Jeffers, Ph.D.

Chapter Two

The Unexpected

We had gotten Ashley to the hospital as requested and remained strong through the preparations. We didn't want her to see or feel our fear, because we wanted her to remain brave and strong. Watching her go through those double doors to the OR was like watching a slow-motion scene from a movie. It didn't feel real. I let go a river of tears.

I implanted that memory of my little girl in my mind. Her ponytail was swinging as she was smiling and waving back at us. I wanted to remember that moment in case, well … just in case. Tim and my mom and I hugged each other and wept in each other's arms. The moment we had been preparing Ashley for was finally here. And there was absolutely nothing more we could do for her at this moment but pray and wait.

I asked God to protect our little girl, watch over her, and help her through this. But most of all, selfishly, I asked that He bring her back to me just like she was when she was wheeled into the operating room. *Just as she was.*

We went to the tiny private waiting room designated for the heart surgery patients' families to endure the excruciating process of waiting. Everything was beyond our control now. Tim and I were accompanied by my mom, affectionately known as Grandma Sharon, my dad, brother, and his girlfriend. Nicole was at home with our nanny Mica and would join us later when Ashley was awake. And then there were the family and friends that were there with us "virtually" through the online journal.

I had made my first online journal posting the morning of the surgery. Little did I know that this would be one in a series of entries that would persist for sixty-three consecutive days and still be occurring four years later.

Day 1 (June 19)
9:30 a.m.

Little girl on a mission

It's almost 9:30 now and Ashley is still being prepped for the heart surgery. She woke up this morning, a little girl with a mission! I woke her up at 5 a.m. and asked her if she was ready for her big day ... she looked at me very calmly and said "Yup." She got up, walked downstairs and was ready to go. I am in "awe" of how calm, peaceful, and mature she was this morning.

I got this incredible feeling that she wasn't alone, but rather being guided along by angels. And again on the drive to the hospital, I had this feeling that we were floating as if on angel's wings. It's hard to explain, but there was just this feeling I had.

Ashley was in good spirits and quite popular this morning with the doctors. She was impressed that so many people were coming by to talk with her on her special day! We got to the hospital at about 5:30 a.m. We snuggled and watched Dora while she got checked over. At about 6:45 a.m. her nurse, Jan, gave her the "giggle juice" medicine to help her feel sleepy. It tasted pretty bad and made her a little nauseous at first, but eventually took effect.

A few minutes later she was playing with the flavored gas masks like they were sunglasses! Go figure! She kept exclaiming "yahoo, yahoo, yahoo." I wish they could have given me some of that giggle juice!

We changed into her pretty blue hospital pajamas, and then the surgery nurse came to give Ashley a ride on the big bed. She willingly rode on the bed (something she's never been willing to do). And was smiling and giggling all the way to the surgery room. We had to say "goodbye" with kisses and hugs at the "magical doors" of the surgery room. Ashley handled it with more poise than her mom, dad, and grandma combined. And we watched her roll through the big double doors with her ponytail swinging back and forth, and she was greeted by everyone in the OR. She waved and smiled.

The heart surgeon has been by to talk with us (we jokingly asked if he got a good night's sleep, he said he did!). The pulmonologist came by after the bronchial scope was done (an extra precaution due to Ashley's history of having the trach). He indicated she was doing well and his tests were all very good.

So about now they should be getting her ready for the surgeon to begin his very important work.

We'll provide more updates in the next few hours. Now we just have to wait and pray.

Love,

Sondra, Tim, and Ashley,

and our family that's here with us.

This was a time when smart phones weren't yet popular and Facebook didn't exist. The concept of telling details of our personal medical journey with our daughter for everyone to read was kind of new to me. I truly expected this online journal to exist for a couple days as a way to keep friends and family informed of Ashley's progress rather than having to make phone calls to people.

For some reason I felt a sense of obligation to keep the communication lines open to all the wonderful people praying for us. I had no idea that what was about to happen would mean that this online journal would become a lifeline for me. So every update and step along the way, with my laptop in tow, I would post an update. After all, we were going to have the agony of waiting for several hours, and it would give me something to keep my mind occupied.

Little girl on a mission

Surgery nurse just called. Ashley is stable and fine. All IV lines are in. Surgery just began.

Sondra

In between updates from the medical team, we sat together in that tiny room. Occasionally, I would walk out to the lobby area and sit by the little waterfall. It felt calming and soothing. I prayed and thought about happy times. We counted down the minutes. My mind could only imagine what was happening at that moment to my little girl. I trusted that she was in the best of care and this would all be over very soon. I just kept thinking that I needed to be patient and soon we would be sitting by her bedside admiring her new "zipper" scar and watching her favorite movies.

Day 1 continued
11:45 a.m.

Little girl on a mission

Just got update ... Ashley still stable and doing fine. We are looking at a couple more hours. The initial plan was to replace the pulmonary valve. The heart surgeon was anticipating they would be able to do this without stopping her heart, in conjunction with the heart bypass machine.

However, he detected some narrowing/compression on her aortic artery (which he mentioned to us previously as a possible concern). So he is doing some repair on that and finishing the placement of the new valve. This meant that they had to stop her heart to do this. This is normal process, but means they must take a lot of additional steps and precautions for her safety.

She's in good hands and the good news is that the doctors are taking the right steps to do this repair in a manner that will be most beneficial to Ashley in the long run.

We are all hanging in there. Please keep the prayers and positive thoughts coming!

Sondra

Ashley had been on the heart-lung bypass with her first heart surgery. So this news didn't really concern us all that much. It felt like it was unfortunate because it was adding additional time and risk to her procedure. But we were grateful that her medical team was addressing all the issues now that could help her thrive and be healthy in the future. It just meant a little more waiting before we would see her.

Day 1 continued
1:35 p.m.

Little girl on a mission

Just got update. Ashley's surgery is done! She's off the heart bypass machine ... waiting to talk to surgeon.

Sondra

One of the nurses had come in to tell us that Ashley's surgery was complete and we immediately rejoiced! We were thinking that the hard part was over and she was now out of the woods.

Everything that was "routine" was falling into place. I was already beginning to visualize the next few days of hanging out in the hospital, followed by a continued recovery at home.

Suddenly everything drastically changed when the surgeon walked back into the room.

The surgeon began by telling us that some complications had developed as Ashley was coming off bypass. He didn't know for certain, but there was a chance there could have been an air bubble that escaped the bypass filters and may have affected oxygen to Ashley's brain. He was explaining that an air bubble could go to the brain and cause a stroke. And that was their concern.

They had done a CT scan and saw nothing and were now doing an MRI to see if anything showed up. I remember it taking him a long time to tell us what had happened. At first I was thinking, *Okay, no problem; a little complication. Her heart's been fixed. She's off the bypass. They are just taking extra precautions. Maybe this will just add a little time to her recovery. She will be fine.* I remember so badly just wanting this "routine procedure" to get over with so I could go hold my baby girl.

But the overall tone and demeanor of her surgeon was suddenly very different. He was almost grave and sorrowful. And then he looked at me and said the words that I will never ever forget, "This is a heart surgeon's worst nightmare."

And at that moment I thought, *Okay, this is serious.* He would have never said those words if there wasn't something significantly wrong.

My head dropped into my hands and I began to cry. And then he reached out and hugged me. And I thought to myself, *Oh my God, there is something terribly wrong.* He had never hugged me before. It was as if he knew that, as her mother, I was about to experience the most painful truth. My body was overcome with fear rushing through my veins.

I wanted to run to Ashley's side. How could this be happening? And the energy of the room completely shifted. I cried uncontrollably when he left the room. Our world had just been shattered. And we would enter a whirlwind of events to try to get our girl back.

We waited for the nurse to come back and tell us what was happening next. I made one quick online journal post. I had just posted that everything was fine and surgery was over and I feared that everyone that was praying would go back to their day thinking they didn't have to pray anymore. And I knew we were going to need those prayers! I had to let everyone know to keep the prayers coming!

Day 1 still not over

5:16 p.m.

Little girl on a mission

We are calling for more prayers. Some complications developed as Ashley was coming off bypass. We don't know for sure but there is a chance there could have been an air bubble that could have affected oxygen to Ashley's brain. The Drs have done a CT scan and saw nothing, now doing MRI. We are hoping and praying that this is nothing to worry about. We should hear more soon ...

Sondra

We soon learned that, although the CT scans and MRI tests were not showing any signs of damage, Ashley may have had a seizure as the anesthesia began to wear off. This would be a signal that, in fact, she had experienced a stroke and her brain had been traumatized.

We suddenly shifted from a routine procedure to repair a heart valve to a situation where we were dealing with potential brain damage. Neurology specialists were now consulted and a recommendation was made to transfer Ashley to The Nebraska

Medical Center for a very special treatment in a hyperbaric oxygen chamber to help flush out any remaining air bubbles in her bloodstream or brain.

We were told that an air bubble could cut off the flow of oxygen to her brain, potentially causing permanent damage. Time was of the essence, and she needed to be treated as quickly as possible. The ambulance was being called to transport her immediately.

We were taken back to the operating room recovery area where Ashley was being prepared for the transport to the hospital on the campus of the University of Nebraska Medical Center. We were able to see our sweet girl's face, kiss her on the cheek, and whisper in her ear that we loved her.

The atmosphere was calm yet rushed and full of looks of concern. It was clear to us that this was not supposed to happen and most certainly not something that happens very often. The anesthesiologist was honest with us and shared with us that she thought Ashley had experienced a seizure. She was concerned yet optimistic that the treatment at the medical center would help her.

Within moments, she was whisked out the doors and into the ambulance. It had just been moments since her chest was being stitched back together from her heart surgery. We were supposed to be greeting her in her hospital room at this moment, but instead we were on our way to another hospital and completely unfamiliar territory. I wanted so desperately to ride in the ambulance with her. However, because of all the post-op support that needed to accompany her, Tim and I had to drive separately. The drive over to the medical center was a blur and all I wanted was to find Ashley and be by her side.

We arrived at the medical center and sat in a waiting room for what felt like an eternity before we were allowed to go into the ICU to see Ashley. She was resting and peaceful. I would whisper in her ear that I was there and loved her, not knowing if she could hear me. We had now ventured into the complete unknown. We were running a marathon without knowing how many miles we would have to run to get to the finish line or what the finish line would look like. There was no way in the world that I could think of leaving Ashley's side. We just had to ride this out.

Amazingly, friends and family stepped into action to do what was necessary to take care of arrangements with Nicole. The original plan had been for me to sleep over with Ashley, while Tim went home to tend to Nicole. We were going to play it by ear and wait to bring Nicole to see Ashley until it would be safe emotionally for both of them. We didn't want Nicole to be scared by seeing her sister in a position that she might think was harmful.

But now, what were we going to do? I remember thinking, *My poor little baby girl is at home missing her sister and her mom and dad and wondering what's going on.* I couldn't bear the thought of having to tell Nicole that her big sister was in trouble, yet I knew that the situation was serious and best for Nicole to be shielded from it until we could get some answers. I wanted to be there for her and give her hugs of reassurance, but I knew I needed to be strong for Ashley. I needed to be strong for all of us.

The concept of the hyperbaric oxygen chamber at first seemed crazy. How could lying in a glass tube with oxygen being pumped in help my daughter's brain? Was this some experimental, back-to-the-future gimmick or would it really work? Has this worked for anyone else that's experienced Ashley's issue? This didn't appear to be a routine procedure. We had so many questions and yet we were at the mercy of the medical professionals to do whatever it took to bring our daughter back to us.

The process of getting Ashley prepared for the oxygen treatments was painstaking and time-consuming. Every single tube and wire that was hooked up to her body had to be switched out before the treatment and then again after the treatment. And at this point, she had numerous tubes and wires hooked up to her. Apparently the high pressure of the oxygen chamber would cause the tubes that were typically used to collapse. Therefore, they had to be replaced with special tubing. It literally took hours to get her ready, hours to be in the chamber, and hours to get her back to recovery to rest.

The room that contained the hyperbaric oxygen chamber was very small. Once Ashley was safely enclosed in the glass chamber, a nurse would monitor her constantly. They were always checking her vitals and IV lines. It was mind-boggling the number of tubes and cords that were hooked up to her. And she was still in a "post-op" recovery state, with a fresh new six-inch wound on her little chest.

This became a nightmare of waiting and wondering. We set up "camp" in a small waiting area right off the elevators. Family and friends would appear as the elevator doors opened and seek us out for a quick embrace. There was a lot of tension and concern. None of us had expected to be in this place, and we were all just adjusting to the shock.

A stroke ... an ambulance ride ... transfer to a medical center ... hyperbaric oxygen. It was surreal! I sat down to write an update on the online journal. I knew family and friends were waiting and wondering what was happening. How would I even begin to explain what was happening?

Day 1 never ending

10:24 p.m.

Little girl on a mission

Lot has happened the last couple hours ... whirlwind. The MRI results did not show anything negative. This was a good sign. However, as Ashley began waking up a little, the anesthesiologist thought she may have had a seizure. They are not entirely sure, but are taking every possible precaution to ensure there are no injuries to her brain.

So she was transported to the Med Center by ambulance. Here's the real adventure that Ashley will have fun telling everyone about ... she is going deep-sea diving! Yes, that's right. She is receiving a "hyperbaric oxygen" therapy. This is a pressure treatment designed to eliminate any air bubbles floating around in her bloodstream. Interestingly, this treatment is given to deep-sea divers who have surfaced too fast, or skydivers, or other such brain injuries.

So our little princess right now is lying in a little bed with a glass bubble around it (looks like a tanning bed with a clear glass top). She looks like "sleeping beauty." The pressure is lowered to simulate a depth of 66 feet below sea level. The point of this is to flush out the air bubbles. We expect this to take another hour or so. Then they will be moving her to a room in the pediatric ICU here for the night. They will pull back on her meds and let her begin to wake up. And then observe.

We won't really know if there is an issue until she begins to wake. They'll watch for seizures or numbness or any other issues. If necessary, they'll do another oxygen treatment tomorrow.

Right now she is stable. Heart and lungs are functioning well, although she is still on the ventilator. The anesthesiologist and cardiac surgeon are still with her. They have been with her since 7 a.m. this morning and are 100% committed to ensuring she comes through. We got to see her a couple times. And she really looks good—very peaceful, good color.

We are surrounded by family. We can't tell you how much your messages and calls of support mean to us. This online journal has been a lifeline for us! It's been a roller coaster day (and not sure what the next turn will be). We are hanging in there.

Many of you know that I am a firm believer in "The Secret" ... the power of positive thinking. So in my mind this online journal is drawing all the prayers and positive energy to help Ashley be strong. So thank you! Keep them coming.

We'll try to post an update later or at least in the morning.

Love and Prayers,
Ashley, Tim, Sondra, Nicole

P.S. Little sister Nicole is in good hands having a little "sleep-over" with nanny Mica.

We were allowed occasional moments in the room with Ashley, one or two people at a time. As Tim was inside checking in on her, I was standing outside in the hallway. I noticed Ashley's heart surgeon looking in on her. I could tell he was in deep consternation. As he rubbed his temples, I heard him say under his breath, "I just don't know how this could have happened. I don't know how the bubble got past the trap."

Ashley's surgeon was a gentle, soft-spoken, kind man. I have always respected him and felt a strong connection between him and our family. After all, he is the man who has held my daughter's heart in his hands. I have always thought about that whenever I have shaken this man's hand.

What I saw at this moment was a man who was deeply sorry for the fact that this had happened. I could only imagine what was going on in his head as he was trying to back-track to figure out if something could have been done to prevent this.

It was nearly midnight, and he had now been by Ashley's side since first thing this morning. He could have walked away and said, "Oh well." But he didn't, he cared about his patient and he cared about the fact that she had a family that loved her and was in anguish. I sensed there was a commitment to do whatever it took to help Ashley through this. I was reassured knowing that he was there with us.

Day 1 continued
11:13 p.m.

Little girl on a mission

Ashley is done with the oxygen treatment. She's now in her room. The doctors decided to keep her sedated and on the ventilator for the rest of the night. Let her rest and wait until morning to let her wake up. She'll be seen by neurologists in the morning and we will go from there.

Love and Prayers,
Sondra, Tim, Ashley, Nicole

With Ashley resting calmly after the first hyperbaric oxygen treatment, we finally sat down in the waiting room to reflect on the day. We were still in shock. It was so hard to believe that this had actually happened and so hard to accept. At this point there was nothing we could do. Time would tell and we would follow Ashley's lead and take the advice given by her medical team about what to do next.

How could this have happened? was the main thought running through our minds. It truly had been an exhausting day. This had been a day from hell.

I was committed to keeping vigil and not leaving Ashley's side. I desperately wanted her to open her eyes and know I was there and give me some signal that she was going to be okay. She had opened her eyes a couple times and each time I was right there by her. But I really don't know if she knew what was going on. The nurses said that she was still heavily sedated.

I remember saying, "Mommy is right here by your side. Everything is going to be all right." I looked into her eyes and was searching for the Ashley that I know. Whenever she woke up, I was determined to be there.

Everyone had gone home and I was going to try to rest for a while in a reclining chair in the waiting room. It was quieter, as there was still constant activity and monitoring going on in the ICU with Ashley and really nowhere comfortable to sit, much less sleep. So I knew I would only be a few steps away and made it very clear to the ICU nurses that they were to come get me if anything happened.

Before closing my eyes to rest, I prayed that this would all be over tomorrow and our daughter would come back to us.

Life Lesson: Everything Happens for a Reason

If there's one single, most important lesson I've taken away from this experience, it's the unshakeable belief that everything happens for a reason. This goes back to the earlier point that "we are not in control." If we believe that to be true, then perhaps there really are no accidents in life.

If we can treat each experience, whether good or bad, with a philosophy that we are supposed to learn and grow from that experience then that's exactly what will happen. It doesn't mean we won't experience all the emotions that accompany that event in our lives. It does mean that we will be able to put it into perspective, make the choices and changes that are necessary, and move forward in a new direction.

As we coped with this event in our lives, I realized that there were people who were placed in my life so that they could help me cope with this tragedy. There was a business opportunity that had been placed in my life to give me an option to care for my family in a different way. New people entered my life because it would become part of how we used this experience to teach and help others. And there was knowledge that I had gained in my life that I needed in order to cope with this event.

We could have continued to look at the situation and ask "why?" Or we could exchange that thinking and embrace that it was a catalyst for us to reset the priorities of our family and shift from a career and lifestyle that wasn't serving us. And use it as a way to teach and help others that might encounter tragedy. We could show our children that nothing that happens in life needs to limit your potential and that truly anything is possible.

Coping Strategies: Rely on Faith

Whether you are a faith-based person or not, I believe that when conquering tragedy you must draw strength from a higher power. If you accept that things are not within your control and there are no explanations for why certain tragedies occur, then you also have to accept that there is a higher power that can set things right. I think it makes it easier to embrace the things that we cannot control or change.

The most prevalent emotion that I remember experiencing was fear. I believe that the antidote to fear is faith. I've always appreciated the expression that you can't wring your hands and roll up your sleeves at the same time. Let go of things that don't matter. Focus your energy on faith.

❝ Be not afraid, only believe. **❞**

— Mark 5:36

❝ He will shield you with his wings. He will shelter you with his feathers. His faithful promises are your armor and protection. **❞**

— Psalm 91:4

Chapter Three

Breakdown

Day 2
12:17 a.m.

Gonna be a better day!

Ashley is stable and resting calmly. She is still sedated and asleep. We've seen her open her eyes a few times, but the doctors are keeping her sedated.

She had an EEG this morning to measure her brain activity, and the neurologist was in to visit with us. She will have another MRI this afternoon. In the meantime our little "sleeping beauty" gets to go deep-sea diving again!! Everyone agrees that it would be beneficial to do another hyperbaric oxygen treatment, so at 11:30 a.m. she'll be going back to her little bubble for a couple hours.

So here's our source of optimism ... we had a nice visit from one of the specialists in the hyperbaric treatment area. He was a very nice, positive, encouraging man. He told us about a little boy a couple weeks ago with the same air brain embolism issue following a heart surgery. They did the treatments on him, and he has recovered completely and is now playing Nintendo!

His advice to us was to be patient and positive and just keep hanging with her. It might take a day or two or a week, but kids heal fast and are incredibly resilient. As he said, kids are not as "cynical" about being sick as us "older" people are!!

I stayed with her last night and got a few naps in, and Tim and the family went home for a brief night's sleep. So we are all doing okay today.

Just keep the prayers coming and think positive, positive, positive!!

Love,

Sondra, Tim, Ashley and Nicole

Despite some feelings of encouragement early in the morning and a feeling that it was a new day, the nightmare seemed to only continue. Perhaps the stress had started to take its toll as reality was setting in. And the lack of sleep certainly wasn't helping. But I was her mother and I needed to be there for her.

And as her parents, we were in charge of Ashley's care. It had become our job to make sense of what the doctors were telling us and ask questions and make decisions about her care. We were experienced in asking questions and translating the medical language into something we could understand. After all, we had already been through six years of cardiologists, pulmonologists, and other specialists.

We were about to discover that the field of neurology and the complexities of the brain did not provide clear-cut answers to what was happening inside Ashley's brain or what was about to happen next. The more questions we asked, the more we heard, "We just don't know. We'll just have to wait and see." I couldn't stand the waiting! I wanted answers and I wanted my daughter back!

Tim and I were both tired and feeling the stress of the situation. We had begun to become irritable with each other. At a moment when we needed to be pulling together and supporting each other, I felt that we were pulling away from one another. We were each trying to deal with this situation in our own way. At one point, Tim grew very frustrated with me regarding my posting of the online journal messages. We were sitting in the back of the ICU room where doctors were tending to Ashley. I had picked up my Blackberry phone to look at a message that had popped up.

"Put your damn phone and computer away. Why do you think you need to be doing that now? I need you here with me," he snapped.

"I have to post the updates. It's for Ashley," I replied angrily.

"That's not going to help Ashley right now," he shot back.

"You don't understand," I pleaded. "I have to post the updates because people are praying for her. And we need them to keep praying for her. She needs their prayers." I had become emotional now.

"We are both trying to cope with this situation as best we can," I told him. "The way I choose to cope may not be the same way you choose to cope. Posting the online journal updates is not only bringing forth prayers for Ashley, it's helping me cope."

Tim took a moment to process the encounter that had just happened. He looked at me and shook his head. He let down his guard and quietly whispered, "Oh, I see. I understand."

And I finally felt that Tim accepted that I wasn't some crazy workaholic, uncaring woman who wanted to play on the computer with my friends. I was searching for encouragement and prayers for our child. Somehow in my mind I knew that it was going to take all the faith and heavenly power possible to heal my child. I had also discovered that what started out to be a fun little message board for Ashley had become my lifeline, my prayer line. It had become my way to cope with the surreal nature of what we were experiencing.

Tim and I were both struggling through our pain and exhaustion. And the challenges of the day seemed to be increasing. We thought we had experienced our worst nightmare yesterday. How could today possibly get any worse?

As the sedation had decreased and Ashley tried to awaken, the seizure activity had started to increase. This was a clear indication that there was damage and her brain was trying to heal. I was in horror as I watched my child lying there asleep, when suddenly her eye or cheek would start to twitch uncontrollably … a seizure. And it would be accompanied by "spikes" on the monitor that was tracking her brainwave activity. We watched and prayed that it would stop.

♥ ♥ ♥

Tim and I accompanied Ashley and her medical team as they rolled her down the hallway for the MRI test, which was intended to get a picture of her brain to give everyone some answers about what was causing the seizures. As we were rolling through the hallway, she began having a significant seizure and I screamed out to the nurse. All we could do was watch and pray that it would stop.

This time her body was convulsing uncontrollably and she was thrashing about. Her eyes were rolling around in her head. A grand mal seizure, much like someone who has epilepsy would have. I had wanted to see her open her eyes and look at me, but not like this. Her eyes were open; however, it was an involuntary reaction of her body to the seizures. This was excruciating to watch our sweet girl as her body was fighting itself. We were not able to do a thing to help her. The doctors assured us that the MRI would hopefully give us some answers.

We waited outside the MRI room. For the first time, Tim and I sat next to each other and cried and held each other. We were trying to deal with the panic that had become part of our reality. Our world had been shattered.

As we sat there waiting, I began to fiddle with my cell phone that was in my pocket. And I realized that I had a voice message on my phone from Ashley. It was a message she had left for me when I was away from home on business. I showed it to Tim. Our eyes locked as I clicked the button to listen to the message. The voice of our sweet, giggling little girl filled the hallway: "Mom, this is Ashley. When are you coming home? I miss you. I love you. Goodbye."

At that moment we longed for her to come back to us and the outlook was starting to feel very bleak as the day progressed. Our hearts were filled with despair. And together we cried for our sweet daughter to return to us.

Day 2 continued
7:06 p.m.

Gonna be a better day

This will be a quick update. We know so many people are hoping and praying for Ashley. We are here sticking it out with her. We were warned this morning that it could be a challenging day. And it has been.

Unfortunately, once Ashley was moved to the hyperbaric therapy room she began having seizures and so the therapy could not be given. She has had several more seizures and the EEG monitoring is showing spikes that indicate seizure activity. She is in MRI right now. We are hopeful that when the neurology team reviews the EEG and MRI results they may be able to see something definitive this time.

We have been continually reminded that we just need to be patient and strong and give her time. A good way to think about this is like getting a bruise. You bang your leg but don't see the bruise until later. It's the same thing here. That little air bubble could have bounced around and caused some damage that is just now showing up. And the seizures, as explained to us, are evidence of "cerebral irritability"—in others words, it's the body signaling that something is not okay there.

We remind ourselves every minute that these are only momentary setbacks and that given proper time her little brain can heal and recover. (People survive severe head trauma every day, even though the journey to get there may be challenging!)

So much for brief! Hopefully this gives a little glimpse into the situation. Ashley is stable as far as her heart and breathing. So we are just trying to regulate the seizures and get a handle on what's causing them.

Keep praying! Positive! Positive! Positive!!

We will try to provide some updates later if we can.

Love and Prayers,
Tim, Sondra, Ashley, Nicole

We accompanied Ashley back to her room in the ICU and continued our vigil of waiting. The ICU room was designed to provide access to the medical team to work on the most acute patients, so there wasn't much accommodation for family to sit. The doctors were trying to minimize the stimulation to Ashley's brain, so we were asked to only have one or two of us in the room at a time.

The lights were dimmed to try to help calm her. I was standing in the corner of the room where I had full view of Ashley and the medical team. I was feeling hopeful because the neurologist had come in to check on Ashley. Surely he would have some answers. He would be able to assure us that this nightmare would soon be over. That our daughter would pull through this and everything would be perfectly fine. I needed to hear that from him so that I could continue in the state of optimism for which I had been desperately striving.

His attention was focused on the monitor that showed her brainwave activity. At this point, Ashley was being given several types of anti-seizure medication and so some of the outward signs of seizure had subsided. But the constant, erratic dance of activity on the brainwave monitor showed very clearly that her brain was in a state of constant seizure. This was a signal that her brain was experiencing trauma as a result of the tiny air bubble that had penetrated her brain.

There was no longer any doubt about whether the air bubble had made its way to her brain. The only question was whether it had lodged in a vessel and cut off the flow of blood and oxygen to the brain, or perhaps the bubble had bounced around and caused damage to her brain tissues. In either case, it had become apparent that something very bad had happened inside her beautiful little head.

I watched the neurologist as he intently studied the monitor and would then take note of Ashley's responses. She was heavily sedated at this point, but there would still be twitches of her eye or face that would be visible in coordination with the spikes of seizure activity on the monitor. The neurologist was instructing the nurse to increase the amount of coma-inducing drug.

As the amount of drug entering her body was increased, the number and length sharpness of spikes on the monitor would diminish. However, they weren't disappearing, which was what needed to happen in order for Ashley's brain to recover. The seizure activity needed to be controlled.

I watched this interaction between the neurologist and other medical staff for some time. My eyes moved back and forth from the monitor to Ashley to the expressions on the doctor's face. I was trying to make my own interpretations of what was showing up on the screen and the resulting decisions being made by the doctor. I could tell that he was not seeing that a satisfactory result was occurring with the incremental increases in medication.

I began to feel a sense of panic. Why is it not stopping? What if it doesn't stop? What if? The thought was too painful to accept. As I retreated farther into the corner I had this horrible, ominous feeling.

The neurologist was so intent on trying to reach a state that he felt was safe for Ashley. And as I had seemingly vanished into the corner, I think he forgot I was in the room. What I witnessed next will stay with me forever.

The doctor repeatedly turned to the nurse who was administering the IV medication instructing her "more." He would study the monitor and turn to her again, "More." After about the third time he said, "We are just going to stop the brain activity altogether in order to allow the brain time to rest and heal." And as the medication was increased, the brainwaves became flatter, and flatter, and flatter ... until there were no more waves. Flat line! Just one steady flat line. My daughter had no brainwave activity whatsoever.

I felt fear! I felt panic! I wanted to escape from that dark little corner and run screaming down the hallway like a mad woman! No! No! No! This can't be happening! My daughter was alive. Her heart was working perfectly. But now she had no brain activity.

Would this end up like the stories you hear about? The stories in which people are kept alive by machines, but they aren't really living. Oh my God! Why did this have to happen? Please, God, bring her back! Please! Memories of her smiles and giggles flashed through my mind. Would I ever experience that again?

Suddenly, the doctor turned to us. He must have seen the look of horror on my face. I had just witnessed my daughter's brain activity be reduced to nothing. He explained to me why this was necessary and how it would give her brain the opportunity to fully rest without trying to do any processing. Rest was what she needed the most right at the moment.

I could barely muster the words to ask the questions that were on my mind: "What happens then? Will her brain activity come back? How will you get it back?"

He explained that she would be in this drug-induced comatose state for probably a couple days and then they would gradually reduce the coma-inducing medication. And then, we would just have to wait and see. In the meantime, he said, all you can do is hope and pray for the best.

I thought to myself, *HOPE AND PRAY!? HOPE AND PRAY?! We are already doing that! We've been doing that for the past thirty-six hours! How can that be our answer! Why can't they fix her brain like they fixed her heart?* I accepted his explanation as calmly as I could, but inside my mind was reeling and I was screaming!

I had to get out of that room. I had to go catch my breath! I felt like I just wanted to die! I wanted my daughter back and I just couldn't deal with the magnitude of what I had just witnessed. The two days of trauma and stress and lack of sleep had taken their toll and I hit my breaking point … literally.

When I think back to these two impossible days, I remember that we were searching to make sense of what had happened and searching for hope. We wanted to have a sense of optimism, but at the same time the gravity of the situation was pulling us down.

It had been two full days since the nightmare began. I hadn't been home. I was still wearing the same clothes I was wearing when we arrived at 5:30 a.m. the day before. I hadn't seen my little girl Nicole. I missed her and wanted to see her desperately. However, Ashley's situation seemed to be getting worse and I needed to be there for her.

Up until this point, I had felt like super-woman. I was strong and I could deal with whatever was dealt to us for the sake of my daughter. After all, we were her parents. Tim and I were responsible for making sure we understood what was going on and could make decisions on Ashley's behalf. There hadn't been time to "fall apart."

Yet the effects of the stress and exhaustion physically and emotionally had begun to take its toll. I had gone back to the waiting room where family and friends were gathered. Tim's mother and sister had come in from out of town. I couldn't talk about how I was processing what I had just witnessed. I needed to keep the calm, positive, optimistic face on. Yet I was absolutely reeling inside.

Tim came in the room and was soon followed by Ashley's surgeon and the neurologist. They had pictures of the MRI results. They sat down at a table with us and they explained that there now was evidence of multiple tiny air bubbles lingering in Ashley's brain. This was the first time we had really had a chance to get some specific answers about what was going on with Ashley.

We asked a lot of questions. Seeing the pictures and hearing the explanation helped us to understand why she was having the seizures. However, the air bubbles had to come out before they caused any more damage. So the medical team was immediately beginning to prep Ashley for another hyperbaric oxygen treatment. We had a plan. As the doctors went back to preparing for the next treatment, Tim went back to be by Ashley's side.

I felt that I needed to take a break and gather my thoughts. I immediately went to the laptop searching for something that would help me shift my perspective. I posted an update.

Day 2 continued
9:33 p.m.

Gonna be a better day

So we now have some definitive results. We just met with Ashley's cardiac surgeon and the neurologist. This time the MRI showed that there are, in fact, numerous tiny air bubbles in Ashley's brain. This is what is causing the seizures. They are not sure why this did not show up earlier or why the hyperbaric oxygen treatment didn't take care of them. The good news is that they are not seeing any indications of damage.

So now we have a game plan, which makes us feel much better. The doctors are increasing Ashley's sedation, basically putting her in a drug-induced coma to stop the seizures. And then they will do the next hyperbaric treatment (which sounds like this will happen pretty soon). They will keep her level of sedation, probably repeat an MRI to see if the air is gone, do more hyperbaric treatments if necessary and just keep at it.

We have a new sense of optimism. She will get past this.

Thank you for the continued prayers and encouragement!

Love and Prayers,
Sondra, Tim, Ashley, and Nicole

P.S. Special thank you to Mica and Matt, Margaret, Sydney, and Ciera Haynes who have been so kind to look after Nicole for us so that we can stay at the hospital and focus on helping Ashley. Nicole is spending a little sleep-over weekend with the Haynes girls ... she will have a blast!

It seemed that when I was forced to describe what was happening to a random group of people who would be reading it at any given moment, I had to be "diplomatic." It probably came from my years of doing corporate sales and customer service and learning how to defuse negative situations or deliver bad news. But then, I have always tried to be a positive thinker.

I wasn't sugar coating. I was trying to deliver news in a way that would help others understand and also that they would be thinking "positive" thoughts. I didn't need sorrow and sadness; I was already feeling enough of that inside. I was searching for ways to combat those feelings.

I read messages from people that encouraged us to dig deep in our faith and pray for everything to be all right.

For all of the family, this has been two very difficult days. So many relatives and friends have been with you all in prayer. I do know that God is listening to all the prayers about how sweet and caring Ashley is for family and friends and how much you all love her. I do believe in my heart Ashley will be okay. I will continue to pray for Ashley and all of the family, at times like this being strong is difficult. My heart goes out to all of you. I am with you each and every day.

Grandma Sharon's friend

My whole church in New Jersey is praying for Ashley.

Sondra's Business Colleague

I am here praying for you and will continue to do so until you are through this. I know Ashley is going to be OK because she is a very strong little girl— just like her mom. As you said, just take it one step at a time and know that we are ALL here praying for you and thinking about Ashley. I know how hard it must be to post the updates but I know everyone appreciates it so we can keep abreast of Ashley's progress. I have to admit, the first thing I did this morning when I got up was to sign on and look for an update.

Sondra's client

Hi Ashley, remember think positive and keep being the strong and brave little girl I know! You will be staying in my thoughts and prayers! Miss You!

Ashley's friend

We are following all of your updates and praying for Ashley and for all of you. You guys are doing an amazing job of staying so positive for your little girl. We wish you love. Stay strong! Ashley can feel your positive energy and she knows how much you all love her. Hope today brings you GREAT news!

Friends

Our prayers come all the way from California thanks to a friend of Sondra's. We all know prayer changes things and with God all things are possible. So your friend asked for prayers for you and your family, that you will get well soon. And when God holds hands with one person through prayers, and they hold hands with others, we are all connected with Him and He hears and answers us. We are praying really hard for your recovery, but we know we must F.R.O.G. **F**aithfully **R**ely **O**n **G**od

Love and Prayers from California

Our thoughts and prayers are with you all as Ashley fights her way through this ordeal. She is strong, resilient and determined. I am confident God will work miracles in your lives. One of my favorite verses is … "He who hath begun a good work in you will see it throughout to completion." God has created an amazing work in Ashley. I can't wait to celebrate with you all as she recovers from this unexpected turn of events.

We are praying for you all and look forward to hearing great news on Ashley's recovery!

Sondra's business colleague and friend

Sondra, simply put …"You are amazing!" I am a mother of a fighter just like you and your strength is an inspiration. The power of prayer can work miracles and I believe it will pull Ashley through this rough spot. If you need a shoulder, an ear or just a hug you can contact me.

Kitty

I only saw you for a second today but you are beautiful! I can't wait until we can play dress-up again and put on makeup what you and Nicole love to do. I am taking very good care of your little sister while you are dreaming of the beach. She asks about you all the time and I tell her that you are taking a long nap. She of course said I don't want to take a nap! We all love you so much and miss your big bright smile! Words cannot describe what you mean to me!

Oxoxoxox

Mica

I was overwhelmed with the support through messages from friends, neighbors, old high school classmates, colleagues, and clients from other states. I was trying so hard to draw strength from all of these encouraging words. One of my favorite messages was a bible verse that would become a guiding force for our journey ahead.

> But Jesus beheld them, and said unto them, With men this is impossible; but with God all things are possible.
>
> — Matthew 19:26

♥ ♥ ♥

I closed the laptop. I buried my head in my hands and I began to cry. This is what I refer to as my breakdown moment. Crying turned into uncontrollable sobs. Suddenly it was all too much to take. I found myself absolutely, totally losing control.

I lost all sense of who was around me or where I was—in a public waiting room at the hospital. It was mostly a small group of our family there, but there were also a few other people in the room waiting for their loved ones. I was sitting at a table in the eating area. I pushed my chair back and fell to my knees. I was losing it! I cried uncontrollably and the emotions took over.

My mom came into the room and was immediately concerned when she saw me. She came to my side, immediately thinking that something terrible had happened to Ashley. For a moment I felt guilty to admit that I wasn't crying about anything that happened to Ashley. I was crying out of grief and selfishness that I wanted my daughter back!

She tried to console me. I tried but it was impossible for me to speak between sobs. Bless her heart, my dear mom was freaked out by me freaking out. As if she wasn't already worried enough about Ashley. Now she had to worry about me too!

About that time, Tim came into the room to tell me they were getting ready to take Ashley to the hyperbaric chamber. When he saw the state I was in, he looked annoyed. As I think back on these events, I know that he was dealing with his own anguish and had his priorities set on being by his daughter's side. The last thing he needed was to deal with a wife that was losing it.

I interpreted his brashness as being "insensitive to me." You see, my husband and I had been married for seventeen years. And despite what everyone might have seen from a distance, we had struggled in our relationship over the past couple years. This isn't terribly uncommon for couples that have a child with special medical needs. Marriage isn't easy anyway and when you add extra complications like that, it can take a toll.

He looked at me and said with a snarl, "Oh, stop it." When I would have expected my husband to come to my side and give me a tender embrace and say, "Honey, it's going to be okay," he did exactly the opposite. I expected him to know what I needed. But honestly, I didn't even know what I needed. I just knew I wanted my daughter back. I was already in a sad state, and so his reaction set me off. I began lashing back.

"Can't you see I'm losing it!" I screamed. "I AM LOSING IT!"

"Just stop it and pull yourself together," he snapped.

I had completely come undone. All the pent-up frustrations and issues I was experiencing in my marriage somehow entered the scene. I had tears streaming down my face and could barely talk but through my rage I could muster a scream.

"Why can't you ever just be there for me when I need you? Why do you always have to be such an insensitive, F****** JERK!"

He looked at me in shock.

"Nice," he said angrily under his breath.

And a slight awareness entered my mind that I had just dropped an F-bomb in front of my mother-in-law and a waiting room of strangers (who quickly exited the room). And then there was a gnawing silence.

Just then the double doors opened from the ICU and Ashley was being wheeled out. It was time to take her to the hyperbaric chamber. I could tell Tim was disgusted with me. And one of us needed to be with Ashley. It was obvious that I was in no state to go with her.

"Now I've gotta go sit there and go through this with Ashley on my own," he said to me in a frustrated tone. And he turned to follow as they were rushing Ashley down the hallway. I later learned that he was upset because he really was worried about me. He had never seen his wife in such a state of anxiety, nor had I ever felt so out of control.

I slumped back into the chair and continued to sob. I began to hyperventilate. I began to feel dizzy and my hands were numb and tingling. I had experienced this feeling once before and I felt as though I might pass out. Someone grabbed a paper bag and held it for me while I bent over to breathe into the bag. Mom had left the room to get one of the doctors.

A very nice, female ICU doctor came in and sat across the table from me. She instructed me to calm down and take slow breaths from the bag. She looked at my mom and suggested that maybe I needed to be taken downstairs to the ER. She was seriously considering that I might also need to be admitted! I think she thought that I was physically in danger. And I have no doubt that I was.

She helped me slowly calm down and gave me some encouraging words that Ashley was stable and fine and that Tim would be there with her. She instructed me to go home and get some rest. I would need to take care of myself so that I could take care of Ashley and what was to come. I couldn't help wondering what would lie ahead.

Slowly I began to regain my breathing and calm down. It was apparent to me that I had really been in trouble and I needed to go home, because I certainly wasn't going to be of any help to Ashley or to Tim in this state. The ICU doctor was adamant that I must not drive and that someone needed to escort me home and keep an eye on me for a while.

Our dear friends, Matt and Margaret Haynes were keeping Nicole for a sleep-over with their daughters, so I didn't have to worry about Nicole. At this moment, I just needed to take care of myself. I succumbed. I called Margaret and told her what was going on. Her sister, a cardiology nurse, would come over to get me and take me home. I was so reassured to have such wonderful women by my side to help me get past the darkest moment in my life.

As I waited, I knew that my need for control and independence was not going to carry me through this time. I realized that this was so much bigger than I. I was scared, because I realized that my sense of optimism had evaporated. It was gone. I was left with nothing but negative, horrible thoughts. I was overcome by darkness. I tried, but suddenly couldn't push these dark thoughts from my consciousness. And it occurred to me that I was going to have to call in every favor from every friend and from God above to get through this.

Two of my closest friends lived on opposite ends of the country, yet somehow I knew I needed them. They understood me. And I knew would help me regain my sources of strength. I called my friend in California. She was vacationing in Arizona with her family. I got her voicemail, "Hello, this is Sondra. If there were ever a time that I needed to call in every ounce of positive support, it is now. I am not coping very well at the moment and I desperately need your help. Is there any way you could come? I would never ask this of you if it weren't really urgent."

I called my friend in Florida. "I know you've been following Ashley's updates. I am really losing it here. I know it's a lot to ask, but is there any way you could come be here with me?"

There was no hesitation in her response. "You got it. I'll make arrangements and be there as soon as I can. Whatever you need."

As I was hanging up the phone, my phone rang and it was my friend from California. She was leaving her family vacation to fly to Omaha. I am forever grateful to those two friends who took a little burden off my shoulders that night. It was my cry for help. And they were coming to my rescue. I needed the emotional support, above all. There were so many others right there by our side. We just needed to learn to lean on them for the support we needed.

♥ ♥ ♥

Margaret and her sister showed up and were full of hugs and understanding. Margaret stayed to comfort Tim. Mom and I went home. I passed on the suggestion that I ride in a wheelchair to the car and agreed that I could walk, although I was incredibly weak.

It felt surreal to be leaving the hospital and Tim and Ashley behind. But I was so exhausted. My legs felt as if they weighed a thousand pounds as I lifted them to get into the car. I was looking forward to a hot shower and some sleep. And I had medication that my doctor prescribed in the event that I needed help sleeping. That needed to be the main priority at the moment. Rest and be ready to deal with whatever would happen tomorrow.

I awoke the next morning feeling some sense of guilt for what happened the night before with Tim and wondering how the night had gone. I immediately called Tim's cell phone. He was hanging in there and was relieved to hear that I had gotten some rest. Margaret had stayed with him for several hours while Ashley was in the hyperbaric chamber. I was so grateful to her for being there as support for him. We both had a little chuckle when we recalled last night's drama.

We were going to be okay. At that moment, I think that whatever marital issues we were having faded into the background. We realized that we were going to have to be strong for each other and pull together, not apart.

After a decent night of rest, a shower, and a change of clothes, I was headed back to the hospital. I had been prepared for several days of hanging out at the hospital with Ashley, but nothing had prepared us for what we were experiencing now. When I arrived back at the hospital, Ashley was being prepped for another hyperbaric treatment.

Day 3
10:54 a.m.

A new day

We are so truly blessed to have such an amazing network of friends and family coming to our support. Thank you!

It just occurred to me this morning, that it's only been 2 days since Ashley began on this journey. It feels as though it's been a year! At least for us. The good news for Ashley is that when she wakes up, she'll think it's still Thursday morning—her special heart day!! This helped me put the last 48 hours in perspective!

Last night I went home and got some much needed sleep. Tim stayed at the hospital last night with Ashley. She did very well with the hyperbaric oxygen treatment (HBO) last night, which concluded at about 3:30 a.m. and then she had a calm night. She is still under deep sedation and getting about 3 different seizure medications. Her brain activity is being monitored by an EEG and it seemed that the seizure activity had subsided.

She will receive another hyperbaric treatment this morning at about 10 a.m. It takes about 4 hours to prep her, move her to the HBO treatment area, complete the "dive" and get her back to her room and stabilized. It is quite a process, requiring a whole team of doctors focused 100% on Ashley. The resilience of these medical professionals is utterly incredible and they are truly committed to getting her better.

And then we'll go from there. The doctors suggested that they'll eventually want to transfer Ashley back to the pediatric hospital, but we'll have to wait and see. They will most likely want to do another MRI to determine whether there is any additional benefit in doing more HBO treatments. The medical research indicates that the greatest benefit of doing these high oxygen/low pressure treatments comes from the first treatment and that the benefits are diminishing with each treatment thereafter. So we are hopeful that last night's 2nd treatment will be the turn-around for her. But we'll just have to give it time and watch the signs she gives us.

Words can't express our gratitude. With all the support we are receiving from this online journal, it feels like we have a "waiting room" full of people right there with us cheering for Ashley's recovery!

Love and Prayers,

Sondra, Tim, Ashley, and Nicole

We tried to think of the treatments in the context of "deep-sea diving" since that's how the treatments are generally used. Ashley was our "little mermaid," surrounded by her little bubble of oxygen and pressure to heal her brain. We imagined that she was dreaming of swimming and seeing beautiful fish "under the sea." We hoped that she was having amazing, beautiful, sweet dreams and would never know of the nightmare that we were all experiencing.

At this moment, she was stable. But she was still in the drug-induced coma with no brain activity. And we still had absolutely no idea what the outcome would be.

We had so many questions. We made a list of our questions, because it seemed to help for Tim and me to talk them through and write them down. We were dealing with such an unknown territory. Who would have ever thought that we would go from interacting with heart specialists to basically dealing with brain trauma?

The field of neurology seemed so vast, so complicated, and so mysterious. And all the answers seemed to be, "We just don't know." It became more and more frustrating!

My brother's girlfriend, Rochelle, was a nurse with experience in this area. She helped us to make a list of medications that were being given to Ashley. There were more than twenty in all, including morphine to manage pain. Strong barbiturates were given to keep her comatose—not to mention the heart drugs and the seizure drugs. I was blown away by the thought of all these lethal drugs being pumped into our little girl's body.

Rochelle also helped us compose a list of questions and encouraged us to request a consultation meeting with the doctors. As Ashley's parents, we felt an awesome responsibility to be her advocates and ensure that she was getting the best care.

I remember sitting in a stuffy little consultation room with one of the neurologists and the nice, female ICU doctor who helped me the night before. She was happy to see that I had resumed a state of mental stability today. She did her best to translate neurological science and put it into the best terms for us to understand. It all still seemed so complicated.

We felt better that we got the chance to ask our questions, yet this was where "faith" was going to have to take over. There was no medicine, no surgery, no "fix" to bring our daughter back. There was only our faith, our love, and time.

We wanted to get all the questions off our minds. We wanted and needed to hear the straight truth. "What happens now?" we asked. The doctors indicated that Ashley's brain would be given time to rest, and then the coma-inducing medications would slowly be removed. And we would just have to wait and see how she responds.

There was one question I couldn't stop thinking about.

"What happens to the brainwave activity? Will it come back?" I asked.

The neurologist looked at me and very apologetically responded, "The worst case would be that it doesn't come back."

Oh boy! I felt the fears coming back to the surface. The tears were building up again. He had just provided confirmation of the darkest, ugliest fears that lingered in the back of my mind.

"I wasn't ready to hear that," I choked out.

Tim put his hand on me reassuringly. We looked at each other. And I knew he felt the same way.

I remember feeling the urge to seek out "information" on the Internet. If the doctors couldn't give me answers, maybe I could find them on my own. When I suggested this idea, my friends immediately warned me not to do that. The Internet is a great source of information, but they feared that I might get the wrong doses of "reality," and they were doing their part to keep me focused on the positive. So, again, I turned to the online journal message board and made a plea.

Day 3 continued
12:39 p.m.

Request for inspiration

I have a request. I know some of you like to surf the web out there! We need POSITIVE stories! Anything you can find on people who have survived brain trauma, beaten the odds, and proven that the power of God and healing is greater than medical science! Post the links or stories so we can read them for inspiration and strength and so we can read them to Ashley to encourage her to fight hard!

Love and Prayers,
Sondra, Tim, Ashley, Nicole

My request was answered and the messages of encouragement began to pour in.

It's a new day, full of new hope. This little girl is full of spirit and fight—keep your spirits high! Remember life is not routine—it is not meant to go according to OUR timeline. Have patience and hang tight together! You are all surrounded by love and prayers—and there is an awesome power in prayers!!

The Mickeys

Our lives are filled with journeys—some happy, some sad, some straight, some crazy zig-zagged. I am sure we all wish we knew why we had to take some of these journeys but ALWAYS know that friends are always there to go with you on your journeys. They may not be there with you physically but are truly always with you. My thoughts have not left you all. I am looking so forward to the email that Ashley is awake and giggling. I am sure I will hear her giggles in my heart! God Bless all of you!

Sondra's college friend

We just want to encourage you to keep praying (as we are also). Ashley is such a sweetie. God loves her more than we can understand. You're in our hearts and minds as we look for words of recovery. Please let us know if we can help in any way (provide food, dog sit, do anything around your house) so you will just be able to spend time with Ashley.

Neighbors

Hi Ashley. We haven't met before, but I am getting to know you through your online journal. Isn't the Internet great! You can easily make friends around the world! I wanted you to know I was thinking about you, and I can't wait to hear about your continued recovery. It sounds like you have a pretty busy life to get back to, full of fun and exciting activities. You will be there soon. You are in my thoughts and prayers. Get lots of rest and get well soon.

New friend from California

Hope sees the invisible, feels the intangible, and achieves the impossible. We are hoping, praying, and believing in the same goal, the power of positive! Thank you to everyone for all your support! It is so neat to see how many people love Ashley. It's what is keeping all of us going.

Mica

Day 3 continued
10:03 p.m.

A new day

Today has been a restful day for Ashley. She has just been transferred from The Nebraska Medical Center to the pediatric hospital in the ICU. At this time, the plan is to maintain the drug-induced coma for several days, let her rest and give her brain time to heal. So she will not receive any further hyperbaric treatments at this point in time. So we just have to be patient, wait, pray, and surround her with lots of love and positive energy!

The decision to transfer her to back to the pediatric hospital is good for all of us. It's a familiar place to Tim and me, as we spent a couple months there with her after her first heart surgery! And for Ashley, she has the best access to the pediatric cardiac specialists and sophisticated care. She's just getting settled in now in room 207.

Once the doctors feel there has been a reasonable period of time passed, they will consider reducing the medications and then evaluate her response. We really will not know anything about her prognosis until that time. This is why it's so important for us to focus on a positive outcome. This little girl is going to pull through this ... I just know that the determination she marched into the hospital with on Thursday morning is the determination that is going to bring her back home to us dancing and singing and giggling!

Please keep the prayer vigils going for Ashley! Now that we are getting her settled into a calmer environment, it will give us time to sit and read the hundreds of wonderful messages to her that you all have sent ... and we know she will hear them!

Love and Prayers,
Sondra, Tim, Ashley, and Nicole

We began to feel as if we were past the life-threatening point. Yet Ashley wasn't out of the woods. She hadn't been awake yet, and I wanted so desperately to see her wake up and smile at me. We still had no predictions of what was going to happen; it was purely a matter of coping and dealing with whatever would come next. With the transfer back to the pediatric hospital, we were able to think about how to settle into a routine of being with Ashley and also of getting back in touch with life at home with Nicole.

Day 4

5:16 p.m.

Nothing but high expectations

We are so happy to have Ashley back at the pediatric hospital. It is just such a warm, child-friendly, and parent-friendly place. The people here have amazing hearts and determination for the families in their care.

It has been a quiet day for Ashley. She is still in the drug-induced coma to allow her brain to rest and heal. The doctors backed off the sedation just a little and we've seen some "bursts" of brain activity. This is a good thing as it shows us there is still an aptitude for brain activity. She was having little "bursts" on her EEG monitor when her daddy touched her and talked to her and when we played her Hannah Montana music! We see this as a sign that she hears us and knows we are here. And she is fighting!

Ashley has had a great "cheering" section for her today! A little "pep rally" to get the positive energy flowing around her. Her mommy's wonderful friends from California and Florida came to whisper in Ashley's ear their encouragement and give some hugs to Mom! And her family and friends have been peeking in on her all day. I know she knows we are all here. We've held hands and prayed and called for the angels that guided Ashley here in such a brave fashion to guide her back to us.

So for now, we will let little sleeping beauty continue to get her beauty sleep. The plan is to let her rest for another 24 hours, and then make a decision about whether to let her start to come out of the sedation.

Keep the positive encouragement, prayers, and energy going! We can't tell you how much we appreciate all the support. We know there is something we are all supposed to learn from this!

Love and Prayers,
Tim, Sondra, Ashley, Nicole

P.S.: Tim says thanks to whoever was so gracious to mow our lawn for us!

Life as we knew it had stopped. What were we going to do about our jobs? It didn't matter. How were we going to pay the bills? It didn't matter. What about other typical errands and commitments? It didn't matter.

Nothing mattered more than getting our daughter back. Nothing mattered more than bringing Ashley home and seeing her and Nicole play together again. Nothing mattered more than just having our family back together. And whatever problems or worries or disagreements we had before this, none of it mattered. We let go of everything and put 100 percent of our energy and focus into Ashley's healing.

Having my friends visit from out of state was comforting. After the moment that I broke down and called them to ask them to come, I felt guilty. But then I let that go. I knew they loved me and wanted to be here to support me. I cherished the brief moments that I could bond with them in the ICU waiting area over a cup of tea. They helped me realize that I was strong and would get through this.

One of my dear friends who had come to visit literally sat for hours "charting" the "bursts" in brain activity that were occurring on Ashley's brainwave monitor. She had a notepad and pen and was recording the time between bursts so that we could share it with the neurologists. It reminded me of charting contractions when you are going into labor. Ironically, we were waiting for the "rebirth" of our daughter. My friend was determined to prove to us that Ashley was working hard at coming back to us.

We were learning to accept all the support and help people were willing to give. There were meals being dropped off to us at the hospital and at home. Friends brought flowers, cards, gift cards, hugs, books for encouragement, and DVD's to watch during the late-night vigils. Nothing was more important than the words of encouragement and prayers. We were overwhelmed by the kindness people showed to us. It's at times like this that you realize how many people you have in your life who really care about you.

Day 5
11:05 a.m.

Today is the day we will get our princess back

Ashley had another peaceful night. Her little brain is resting and healing. Her Grandma Sharon stayed by her side again last night, so Tim and I could go home and get some sleep and spend a little time with Nicole this morning. When Nicole asked this morning, "Where's Ashley," and I told her she's taking a really long nap, she said, "I want her to take a nap with me." She misses her big sister.

We've been surrounding Ashley with music, which she loves. I found a quote this morning that I thought was really relevant:

> *Within each of us is a loving, magical, powerful being ...*
> *a Real Self ... Music, friend that it is, cocoons us*
> *from our worries enabling that hidden self to emerge.*

We are waiting for the doctors to make their rounds this morning. They have turned off the Pentobarbital ... the coma-inducing sedative and are going to let her begin to come out of the sedation (which will take some time ... up to 36 hours is the life of the Pentobarb). We will now watch her closely to see what kind of brain activity is there and how she responds.

Keep the prayers coming and we will keep you all posted.

Love and Prayers,
Tim, Sondra, Ashley, Nicole

For the most part, we were taking turns living in the ICU. Not a moment passed that a family member wasn't right there by Ashley's side. Even though she was not awake to speak to us, we knew that she would know that we were there. We wanted her to be surrounded by the positive energy and love of her family. We took turns staying with her: myself, Tim, Grandma Sharon, my brother, Mike, and his girlfriend, Rochelle. We set up camp and were there as long as it would take!

Day 5 continued
5:59 p.m.

Today is the day we will get our princess back

We are patient and optimistic. Ashley is now off the coma-inducing drug. She remains on a seizure medication and another drug to maintain proper blood pressure, which she will eventually come off as well. We are seeing more and more steady brain wave activity, and so far no seizures. The neurologist indicated that it may take several days for the sedative drug to come out of her system enough for us to see actual movement or for her to wake up.

We are maintaining her little bedside vigil of music and having her family around her. Slowly I've been working on combing the endless tangles from her long blond hair (a by-product of the multiple applications and removal of the brain sensors and all the moving from bed to bed for the various treatments). She will be mad if she wakes up and sees the state her hair is in currently! And we don't want our little princess to be cranky when she wakes!

We will continue to keep you updated on her progress.

I wanted to share an interesting statistic that I read the other day. It is reported that the risk an air embolism to the brain during surgery (like Ashley experienced) will happen is .1%. That's 1 in 1000. So when we thought about this a little more, and considered the number of pediatric heart surgeries conducted at the pediatric hospital, this is a rare occurrence every few years.

So, if something this rare has happened to our princess, we know the odds of miracles happening have got to be greater! And God must really have a special plan for Ashley once her miracle happens!!

Love and Prayers,
Sondra, Tim, Ashley, and Nicole

I remember thinking back to the pre-surgery process. The standard paperwork that we had to sign as her parents authorizing the surgery and accepting the risks of stroke and even death that could occur. At the time, although the words glare at you from the page, you put them out of your mind. You think, *That would never happen to us.* Because what else can you do? And you take a deep breath, and you sign the papers.

Day 6
1:06 p.m.

Ashley's amazing adventure

Ashley is now completely off all the medications. Little sleeping beauty is still sleeping and we are slowly waiting for the drugs to wear off. So far her EEG has been good brain activity. She is getting an MRI right now, and so hopefully from that the neurologists will be able to tell us something about the progress her brain has made in healing.

Tim stayed with Ashley at the hospital last night. I am at home trying to get some rest as I am fighting off a chest cold and don't want it to get worse or to expose Ashley.

I'll post later today if we get results from the MRI or if we see any signs of responsiveness from Ashley. It could still take a while so we remain positive and optimistic.

Love and Prayers,
Sondra, Tim, Ashley, Nicole

Physically the stress had begun to take its toll. Sleeping on the vinyl couch in the ICU waiting room is not the most restful experience. When I started to feel a cold coming on, I knew that I had to try to will it to go away. I wanted and needed to be there with her, but the last thing she needed right now was to catch a cold virus.

So I wore surgical masks when I was near her and washed my hands repeatedly like a maniac. At night, I tried to mask my coughs for fear that the nurses would kick me out and tell me it wasn't healthy for Ashley for me to be there with her. So going home to rest was probably a good idea. But it was so hard to leave her.

Day 6 continued
5:49 p.m.

Ashley's amazing adventure

We just spoke with Ashley's neurologist. The MRI shows there is still swelling of her brain. And there is not really any change from the last MRI. He said this is not unusual, as it is often weeks, not days that are necessary for the swelling to subside.

The most encouraging words he spoke were that he is not seeing anything from the MRI that tells him that the injury that has occurred is irreversible. NOTHING IRREVERSIBLE!! Those words will stick with us. He also said that even if one side of the brain has injury from something like a stroke, that the other side of the brain can find ways to compensate ... even more so in children than adults.

The bottom line is that our bodies and minds are amazing and complex. And Ashley's resilience has never been a doubt in our minds.

Ashley's nanny, Mica, brought us a book and CD yesterday. It has always been one of my favorite songs, sung by Lee Ann Womack. The lyrics are ever so appropriate right now ...

> *Promise me that you'll give faith a fighting chance*
> *And when you get the choice to sit it out or dance*

I hope you dance ... I hope you dance

Ashley, you will dance again! I have no doubt, sweet girl! You will dance!

Love and Prayers,

Sondra, Tim, Ashley, Nicole

Life Lesson: Relationships (and Marriage) Require Work

These days it's easy to give up on relationships. Marriage is not always easy. It requires a lot of work. As Tim would say, "A LOT of work!" Notice the emphasis on LOT! Divorce statistics are very high for couples that have a child with special needs. Take the typical every day stress and add doctor visits, surgeries, long hospital stays, medical bills, disagreements over doctor's recommendations, and you have a formula for even more marital despair.

I will admit that there have been times that I thought my marriage would become one of the statistics. We have had to constantly make the choice to work together instead of against each other. We often don't share the same opinions about what should happen, who to trust or what to do in given a situation.

It's in those moments that we have to show respect. It's a matter of respecting that our opinions may differ. It's showing respect for each other's different ways of coping. And it's showing respect to each other for our different ranges of emotion.

I know one thing for sure. I can always look back on this journey and trust that my spouse always had the best interests in mind with regard to our daughter and the future of our family. Getting through this experience was a lot easier working together than trying to work through it alone.

Coping Strategies: Pull Together, Not Apart

Every individual has a different set of coping mechanisms based on a lot of factors. Some people want to talk and be surrounded by people. Others want to be left alone to process their thoughts. Some people may journal or blog. And others want to just ponder or think inwardly. I believe it's important to talk openly about what each other is experiencing and assess jointly whether the coping strategies are healthy.

Tragic events can often add fuel to relationships that are already strained and create additional tension. However, they can also create an opportunity to mend fences, let go of petty issues, and refocus relationships based on new perspectives.

" When I am sick I will call upon the elders of The Church to pray over me and anoint me with oil in the name of the Lord. And the Prayer offered in faith will make me well; the Lord will raise me up. 'Talitha Cumi' Little girl rise up! "

— James 5:14-15

Chapter Four

Waking Up

Those initial days seemed to go on for an eternity. We expected going into the surgery that Ashley would be sedated and unable to communicate for a few hours and that she would be groggy and cranky once she woke up. But we never expected that we would have to wait for days for there even to be a signal of her waking up and knowing we were there. It was hard not to fill the hours with thoughts of her as we knew her. We cherished all the happy memories like gold now. We hoped that we would be able to create new happy memories again, someday very soon.

I would go home on the nights that I wasn't staying with Ashley and lie in her bed or hug her stuffed animals and smell her sweet little smell that lingered on them. I would lie in bed and cry myself to sleep, longing to be able to snuggle and hold her next to me. She was still in the ICU, on a ventilator, and still not awake. As much as I wanted to crawl right up there in bed next to her, she was just too fragile.

Every day, I kept thinking it would be the day that Ashley would wake up. Somehow, I kept expecting that when the drugs wore off, she would just wake up and then everything would be fine. We realized that the hopes and expectations that we had weren't always in sync with the reality of the situation. Yet it was our way of coping with the situation. I had no idea of the long road that was still ahead, but every day we clung onto any little signal or movement as hope that our princess was finding her way back to us.

♥ ♥ ♥

A dear friend and colleague had visited Ashley and prayed with us. She was like an angel, and I credit her for setting our "expectations" in the right direction.

She took one look at Ashley and said, "She's going to be fine, I just know it."

She sounded so sure, so confident.

"Why do you say that?" I asked, thinking she had some knowledge or observation we had missed.

"Because she is a special child of God and He has a plan for her."

My friend told us not just to "Believe" that God would work a miracle to bring our daughter back to us, but to "Expect" it.

"Expect it!" she said with complete conviction.

And because I was trying to hold onto every ounce of hope I could find, I made a choice to believe her.

A couple days later someone gave me a beautiful necklace that had an engraving on it that said "Expect a Miracle." I put it on and didn't take it off!

We decided that we needed to have absolute positive energy and love surrounding Ashley at all times. So we made a pact that only positive thoughts and people could enter her room. Tim and I began wearing rubber bands on our wrists. They were a symbol to think positive, and when a negative thought entered your mind, you were to snap the band. The sting to your wrist was a signal to stop thinking negative thoughts! There were some moments when my wrist would get rather red from the snapping of the band, and there were moments when Tim and I were snapping each other's bands and trying to keep each other focused on the positive.

Day 7
12:25 p.m.

One more fighting day

Ashley continues to fight her way through recovery. She is slowly waking from her long slumber. She has opened her eyes about half-way (when her daddy said good morning to her)! She is moving her arms and wiggled around when we tickled her feet. She's now breathing over the ventilator, so maybe tomorrow they'll be able to take her off the ventilator.

She's on a morphine drip to keep her comfortable but no more coma-inducing drugs. She's still on a couple seizure control medications, but so far we've not seen any visual signs of seizures. The neurologist will be by later to talk with us again. Ashley's heart surgeon just stopped by to check on her ... he is truly a very caring man.

Another day practicing the virtues of patience and positive thinking!!

Love and Prayers,
Tim, Sondra, Ashley, Nicole

Day 7 continued
10:07 p.m.

One more fighting day

Ashley has made some really great improvements today. The neurologist said her EEG reading looks better today. She is slowly coming down from the high levels of coma-inducing sedative. She still has a ways to go, but she's coughing and breathing over the ventilator ... so hopefully tomorrow they may be able to take her off the ventilator.

She is moving more and trying to open her eyes occasionally. We brought her little sister Nicole in to see her this evening, which was a little scary for

Nicole at first. We thought it would be good for Ashley to hear Nicole's voice and giggles ... motivation to get up and play!

So, we continue to be patient and optimistic. Tomorrow will bring more positive signs!

Love and Prayers,
Sondra, Tim, Ashley, Nicole

During the time that Ashley was stable and her brain was healing, I came to cherish some of the quiet time. I tried to fill the time with reflection, pondering, journaling, reading positive poems and scriptures. I thought about where we were in our family, marriage, and where I was in my life. Where did we want to go from here? It was a time of quiet peace.

Since then, strangely, there have been times I longed to go back to that. Not the fear or pain or misery, but that quiet, peaceful feeling. It was a time when everything melted away and nothing mattered more than the love of our family. Since then as day-to-day life has returned, it's hard to make the time for quiet reflection. I have learned to lower my expectations about life, my career, and of myself. We learned to just simplify our lives and our thoughts.

Fortunately, we had the luxury of our nanny to watch after Nicole during these early challenging days. At night, we would continue our rotating schedule of one of us sleeping at the hospital. It wasn't the most comfortable night's sleep; there was constant beeping and activity checking vitals, IV lines, ventilator, monitors, and medications. I couldn't bear the thought that Ashley would be lying there in a room without one of us nearby, and so one of us was always at her side.

Day 8
1:33 p.m.

A hopeful day

Today marks a week since Ashley's heart surgery. I keep thinking of her waking up today and asking, "Mom, is it still my special heart day?" And we'll say, "Well, it's Thursday!" And maybe she won't even remember anything that has happened the past week.

Today is another day of hope with little positive signs of improvement. The coma-inducing medication is very, very slow in metabolizing from the body. She only dropped from a level of 48 to 44 overnight. The day before was a drop of 6. She probably needs to be in the 30's before she'll become fully awake. She's currently on a morphine drip to keep her comfortable with the breathing tube. Unfortunately, the morphine slows the metabolism of the other medication. This morning the doctors discussed the plan to get her off the ventilator today. So if that goes well, that will be a huge step forward!

She's beginning to move her hand enough now that she appears to be grabbing at the ventilator tube! So we now have to watch her closely to make sure this determined little lady doesn't get mad enough to pull the tube out on her own! The nurses just turned off her feeding tube, which has to be off for 4 hours before they can extubate—remove the vent tube ... so hopefully in 4 hours our little princess will be free of the breathing tube!

We are seeing more movement on her left side, and limited movement on her right side. This could be an indication of some of the brain injury, but it is really too early to tell ... and regardless of what's been affected now, we are optimistic that she will heal with enough time, love, and determination!

My inspirational message for the day:

If you're ever lying on a beach with
80 billion grains of sand beneath you,
700 thousand ocean waves before you,
60 million stars stretched out above you,
and you're still not at all impressed,
I want you to think about this:
The light you see reflecting from the stars is over one million years old.
WOW.

But then, just before you start to feel like a mere blip
in the gigantic scheme of things, please remember this:
Yes, you are small, but you're also irreplaceable
and invaluable
and miraculous.
Those stars don't have anything on you.

They don't have anything on you, Ashley. You are irreplaceable, invaluable, and miraculous!

Love and Prayers,
Sondra, Tim, Ashley, Nicole

Day 8 continued
12:31 a.m.

A hopeful day

Our expectations of Ashley waking up and saying, "Hi, Mom and Dad!" weren't too realistic given that she still had a breathing tube down her throat.

Ashley has been fighting with all her might today. It has been a rough afternoon and evening for our little girl. She fought her breathing tube most of the day, and when we thought she would soon bite all the way through it, her daddy said, "Enough ... get the tube out." We saw it as her sign to us that she was ready.

So at 5 p.m. today, Ashley came off the ventilator. The first couple hours were very stressful for her and for us. We spent a lot of time encouraging her to cough and clear her lungs, hoping that she could keep her breathing and oxygen levels stable enough that the breathing tube would not have to be placed back in.

As of 10 p.m. when Grandma Sharon, Nicole, and I left, our favorite nurses were with her and the respiratory therapists were doing some treatments to see if they could give her a boost with her breathing. Tonight is a key turning point for Ashley. We are going to really pray that she is able to have a restful night. And her daddy is staying there to watch over and protect her (along with all of her angels).

My heart just aches for this little girl that she has to endure all of this. She is stronger than I could ever hope to be. God please give us the strength to continue this marathon journey. And, God bless Ashley's amazing daddy for loving her so deeply and protecting her.

Love and Prayers,

Sondra, Tim, Ashley, Nicole

Watching Ashley fight that breathing tube all day was a horrific thing to watch. I remember thinking how awful that had to feel to have that huge tube shoved down your throat. It's one thing to have it there while you are under anesthesia and don't know it's there; it's entirely different to be awake and have the sensation that something is in your throat and you are being prevented from removing it.

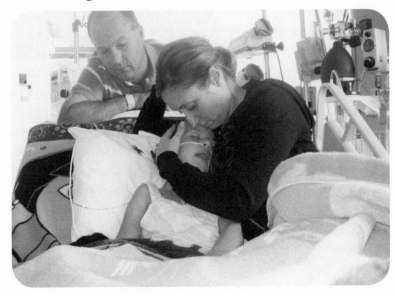

Now that Ashley was free of the breathing tube, we could do more to comfort her. I couldn't resist climbing into bed with her.

It had truly become torture for us to watch. As much as I wanted to trust the medical professionals, I couldn't bear it any longer. And when the time came that Tim boldly demanded as her parent that the tube be removed, I was grateful to him for having the courage to make the decision on her behalf.

Day 9
1:47 p.m.

Another hurdle cleared

"Oh my goodness!" as Ashley and Nicole often say ... we've cleared one more hurdle! Ashley made it through the night being off the ventilator and is doing well. She's still getting some breathing treatments to help her clear her lungs, but she's holding her own!!

She actually got to get in a wheelchair this morning and go for a ride around the ICU floor! And, with nurses as my witness, I BELIEVE she said, "Mom!" I said, "I'll take it!" She still is very sleepy, has limited mobility. She's grinding her teeth quite regularly, but the Drs don't think it's seizure activity, rather, may be some reflection of the injury her brain has experienced.

She just had another EEG reading taken, and we'll consult with the neurologist later. We continue to remain patient and optimistic right now. We may still have a long journey of rehabilitation ahead, but this little girl has made amazing progress so far! She truly is a fighter!

I took some pictures of her this morning in the wheelchair with her EYES OPEN!! I'll post them on the page later tonight once I can download.

We feel everyone's energy and encouragement. I read many of the messages to Ashley yesterday, and we'll read some more to her today.

And, have I mentioned the angels in Ashley's room? Yes, I believe her room, at times, is crowded with angels. There is a sink in the room with a motion sensor on the water faucet. The last few days, especially during some of the most challenging of times, this water faucet turns on by itself ... repeatedly ... with no one even close to it. We've begun to get used to it and we actually feel comforted every time we hear the water run, "There's one of her angels again!" Sometimes I have to say "excuse me" when I wash my hands, there are so many angels in this room!!

Tomorrow is Ashley's 7th birthday! Thank goodness we had her Hannah Montana party a couple weeks ago! So tomorrow we'll have to have a little birthday party for her in the hospital. She loves birthday parties, so hopefully it will motivate her to want to get up and join the party!

HAPPY BIRTHDAY, SWEET BABY GIRL! WE LOVE YOU!!

Love and Prayers,

Sondra, Tim, Ashley, Nicole

At that moment in time, we were clinging on to any small accomplishment. We celebrated every small step of progress. Ashley was alive! She was awake! She was off the ventilator! And for the most part, her body had now begun to function sufficiently on its own. As I look back at those first pictures taken, I am reminded of how distant Ashley actually was from us. That feeling of looking in each other's eyes and "connecting" as mother and daughter just wasn't there yet. I knew she was in there trying to find her way back, but her body just couldn't show us the response we needed and wanted to see. This worried me immensely.

We were gradually getting our daughter back piece by piece. But I also couldn't shake the feeling that we might not ever know her as we had known her before. These are the fears and thoughts that continued to plague us. As I look back at the photos, I understand why that was the case.

There is one photo in particular that I still find rather haunting because it shows how distant and fragile Ashley was. She's in a wheelchair wearing her Hannah Montana PJ's that had to be split down the back so we could quickly take them on and off. She has braids in her hair to contain it. She has a large bandage on her chest from her incision. There are scabs on her forehead, the by-product of having the EEG wires glued to her head. And while she appears to be looking at the camera, her empty eyes seem to stare right past it. It was that look of emptiness that caused us to worry what brain functionality would return and the severity of her brain trauma.

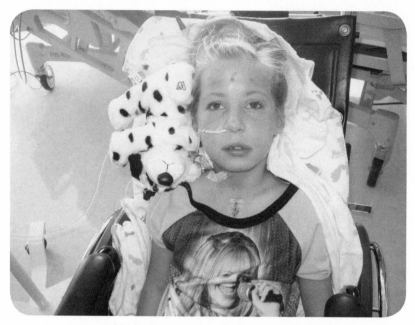

Ashley's empty stare gave us cause to worry.

Yet, we would snap our wristbands and project our thoughts in a positive direction. We would continue to "Expect the Miracles" to happen.

I was also beginning to experience an amazing growth in my faith. We had been good Christians who went to church often. But I honestly had never been in a place like this where faith seemed to be all we had. When there were no other answers, the only thing to turn to was faith.

I accepted that there are some things that we just cannot explain, even though we are all human and our nature is to search for an answer. There was this "feeling" that something really powerful was happening. And we were just floating along day by day trusting that our faith would carry us through.

It was like the feeling that there were angels in the room. There simply was no other explanation for why the water would sometimes just turn on by itself! At first it was weird. And then it became reassuring. I began to visualize the angels in the room and it gave me a sense of peace, and "knowing" that this was in God's hands and He was taking care of Ashley.

When I thought back to the morning we were driving to the hospital for surgery and I felt as if we were floating. I truly believe we were. I truly believe we were being carried on angel's wings. We were, somehow, being gently prepared ahead of time for what was going to happen.

Day 9 continued
1:16 a.m.

Another hurdle cleared

Ashley has even more stories to tell ... like the day she was in the ICU at the pediatric hospital and had to take shelter during a tornado! Yes, that's right! While we took shelter today, we wondered, "Will we have a house to go home to, when this is all over?!" Fortunately, Nicole was with friends. We were in a safe place, and the tornado did not damage our house! But we figured Benny, the family dog, was probably scared at home all by himself!

Much improvement today! The neurologist said the EEG looks much improved over the last one, and Ashley is responding and moving more. She got a shower today! A nice nurse braided her hair. And she got another ride in the wheelchair (to seek shelter from the storm!).

You know the saying that eyes are windows to the soul? Well I believe that now more than ever. Ashley and I locked eyes for what seemed like 15 minutes today. I could feel that happy, silly little girl in there, trying to come back out.

A few weeks prior to surgery, Ashley was telling us about a picture she had drawn at school, and she called it an "illustration." We were quite impressed by such a big word. Then she went on to say that an illustration is "detailed," and when we asked her to explain that, she said that means it's not "random." We were very impressed!

Today, Ashley impressed us even more. She was vocalizing more ... trying to tell us when she needed something! And she would move her left arm more when she was uncomfortable or needed something. It may not have been "detailed" movements or speech ... but it was not random! She is trying to find ways to communicate with us. I am confident that each day will bring small improvements. And a lot of days will mean BIG improvement!

There are some times when a girl just needs her mom! And so tonight, I'm with Ashley. I wouldn't want to be anywhere else than by her side when she needs me. And as I look at the clock, it's past midnight ... and that means it's Ashley's 7th birthday!

HAPPY BIRTHDAY SWEET GIRL!

Love and Prayers,
Sondra, Tim, Ashley, Nicole

I continued to draw strength from the constant prayers and support that came to us through the messages on the online journal.

I'm another heart mom who is keeping up on your progress. While we were in the hospital last month with our 4 month old, another little heart boy brought by some tennis shoes. His doctors told him that a heart life is a marathon, not a sprint. Our prayer for you is that you get stronger each day and that you enjoy your long beautiful marathon that lies ahead of you.

Fellow Heart Mom

What a little super star you are, Ashley! And what wonderful news! All of it signs of a miracle in progress! It is not every day that we get to see firsthand a blessing by God! Thank you for letting us all be a part of it! You are all on my mind, and I am sending a continuous prayer your way! Hugs and prayers!

Sondra's "Expect a Miracle" Friend

As you journey through life, choose your destination well, but do not hurry there. You will arrive soon enough. Wander the back roads and forgotten paths keeping your destination in your heart like a fixed point of a compass. Seek out new voices, strange sights, and ideas foreign to your own, such as rides for the soul. And if upon arrival you find that your destination is not exactly as you had dreamed, be not disappointed. Think of all you would have missed but for the journey there. And know that the true worth of your travels lies not where you come to be but who you became along the way. Ashley, I have always known that you have touched my heart in a way no one else has and because of this my life has truly been blessed. I LUV U Beautiful Girl!

Xoxoxoxo

Mica

Ashley, Sondra, Tim, Nicole, you have every ounce of positive thinking I can send your way. I am praying for Ashley and just know that she is going to be telling her "Superhero" story to her grandkids someday. She has not gone through everything she has already faced without a reason for her to be a positive influence in lives for many, many years to come.

Sondra's work colleague

Hey Ashley. I wanted to let you and your family know that there are thousands of people praying for you from all over the world. My sister works for a motivational speaker and they are holding a conference this week in California. She has asked them all to pray for this sweet little girl in Nebraska. I know you will soon be dancing again.

Sondra's former business colleague

Hey babe, Nicole and I really miss you. Nicole keeps asking about when you are going to wake up from your long nap and how we should go check on you. She has been so brave also but she has had a good teacher, you! We went to get Nicole's hair cut and she brought you home a sucker. I am doing my best to keep Nicole busy and happy while you are getting your beauty rest. Remember the note you wrote me last week that said Mica, I love you. You are very nice and pretty. I read it every day and I am patiently waiting for another one because you make me smile like no one else! All throughout the day we say little prayers for you. It won't be long and we will be playing again! We Luv U Sweetie!

Mica and Nicole

We continue to pray for Ashley and all of you. As I follow your postings I imagine Ashley as a beautiful rose bud, just blooming slowly in the sun every day, with another petal unfolding to give another little glimpse of what's to come of the beautiful full rose again. Each report we get is another wonderful sign of blossoming. You are so right, even if you may see a little weakness from injury, she will rehab so well. As a nurse I've seen children spin circles of recovery around the doctors and therapists. She'll be just fine. God bless Ashley and all of you, we have too much to be thankful for.

Your neighbors

Ashley, your mom may know this. I am a spreadsheet fanatic. Now what does that have to do with you? Well here goes.

There are over 242 messages on your online journal as of June 26, just a week since your surgery. If we consider that some are duplicates from the many friends and family who all love you so much and we use just half of that number to be conservative: 121. We then apply the rule of six degrees of separation. Each person has talked to at least six other people about you and what an incredible young lady you are. Those people have talked to six more. And so on. With the help of a spreadsheet to do the math, you have touched the lives of over 5 ½ million people who are praying and thinking about you, all within a week. Wow!!!

You have touched millions of people across the country and the world.

Sondra's business colleague from Florida

Everyone we know on the East Coast is thanking God in advance for your perfect recovery! We know that great and mighty are the plans that God has in store for you! Blessings!

Tim and Sondra's friend from high school

Hi, Ashley! I am a fourth grade teacher in North Carolina. I was visiting the online journal website because my best friend since ninth grade has a son that has a heart condition and he has an online journal. I was reading yours and am in awe of what a beautiful brave girl you must be. I am sending ALL my prayers and courage your way! Isn't it amazing to know that you touch and make a HUGE impact on people you don't even know! WOW! Keep fighting ... I will continue to read about you every day! May God bless you!

Teacher in North Carolina

I have been following your progress and can't believe how brave and strong you are. God has truly blessed you and your family with the strength to endure. Please remember God will never give you more than you can handle. My family and I are continuing to pray for you every day. I know your family is waiting for the day that you will get up and DANCE again.

Sondra's former work colleague

Ashley and Family, take comfort in the fact that God is with you. I know this time has got to be heart wrenching and you are certainly in our prayers. If there is anything, anything at all I can do, please know I'm here.

A family friend

I read the updates and messages with tears in my eyes. I cannot imagine how hard this is for your family. I know you are a strong little girl and just need some more time to rest before you are ready to get up and go! Be strong. There are a lot of people praying for you and your family.

Business colleague from Kansas City

I'm a friend of a grandmother to another heart child, who mentioned you and your daughter in recent conversations. I was at the hospital visiting them today and I crossed over to check in on Ashley. I just had to tell you what an inspiration you all are! I love the angels in the room and also believe they are watching over your lovely daughter and I will be adding my prayers to the many I sense are already out there. But I wanted to tell you one other thing. I have a 15 year old daughter, and with all the trials and frustrations and fears being the mother of a typically frustrating attitude-charged teenager brings (I won't scare you with horror stories, I'll let you have the joys of experiencing that firsthand with your girls in a few years!). The reminders to cherish the moments and hold your child close and pray over them was a much needed reminder! So thank you for sharing your wisdom and courage and strength with those of us stressing over "non-issues" and reminding us what real priorities should be! May God continue to watch over your family and bring Ashley back strong and healthy and DANCING to the family who believes in her!

A friend of a concerned friend

I closed my laptop and lay down on the vinyl hospital couch, my bed for the night. Our lives seemed for the moment that they didn't belong to us. We were in limbo. We were separated as a family. Ashley was still under constant care in the ICU, and I was sleeping as a "guest" in her ICU hospital room. Our lives had been torn apart and exposed to everyone. The online journal had become my refuge. I was truly amazed at the support that was pouring in from all over the country. As the list of fans grew, it also meant that our lives became more visible.

The morning would bring a special day, a birthday to be celebrated with family and friends at home. Yet here we were. I closed my eyes and prayed that we would all be back at home together very soon.

I had awakened the next morning on the vinyl couch feeling very melancholy. It was Ashley's seventh birthday. When we scheduled her surgery, we expected that she would be recovering at home by her birthday. As a mom, I was feeling guilty that we had planned it this way and my poor baby was missing her birthday. Not to mention Ashley's surgery had also taken place the day of my brother's birthday. I felt bad that something so traumatic occurred on his birthday. We truly had not expected things would turn out this way.

Ashley was awake, but she really wasn't coherent enough to know what was going on. I knew she wouldn't remember today, but I wanted to do something special that I would always remember and cherish this day and my love for her.

As I've continued to point out, I believe things happen for a reason. A couple nights before Ashley's surgery we had gone out to eat at one of Ashley's favorite Mexican restaurants. As we were sitting in the lounge waiting for a table, something caught my attention. A young woman was standing nearby and I noticed a tattoo on her foot. It was a simple inscription of the word *Believe*. I thought to myself that it must have significant meaning to her. I was about to turn to her and ask her when we were called to our table.

In the past couple days, the memory of that tattoo kept coming back to me. I was searching for ways to keep my mind focused on believing that everything would turn out all right. I had the "Expect a Miracle" necklace, the rubber bands, all the books, cards, and online journal messages. Yet I was still struggling. It suddenly occurred to me that I needed a "permanent" reminder to just believe! Mica had been in the room with me as we were watching over Ashley. It had been a moment of vulnerability.

All of a sudden I blurted it out, "I'm going to get a tattoo on my foot of the word *Believe*. I need to have something permanent that will always be there as a reminder to keep believing and have faith. If it's there on my foot, I will see it every single day when I take a shower or put on my shoes."

"I'll do it too!" Mica said.

"Oh my gosh. Really?"

"Yes, and I'll bet your mom would do it too! Tim would too. We'll all go together to do it for Ashley," she suggested.

And sure enough, when I told my mom what we were planning, she said, "I'd get it on my forehead if it meant that it would bring our little girl back to us."

And I had no doubt in my mind that she would do it, if that's what it took.

At that moment, I knew that we were all in this together. We would support each other and get through it together.

So on Ashley's seventh birthday, the four of us ventured over to a local tattoo studio that my brother, Mike, had scoped out for us. While he stayed and kept watch over Ashley in her new hospital room, we took turns getting the word *Believe* inscribed on our bodies.

As I felt the pain of the needle scorching the skin on the top of my foot, I clinched down and held my mom's hand. I felt tears fill my eyes, not because of the pain I was experiencing, but because of the pain that I could only imagine my sweet little girl had endured. And when my mom took her turn in the chair, I was amazed to watch her resolve. She didn't even flinch, and I knew she must have been thinking the same thing I was.

I went into the other room to check in on Tim. He had chosen a more "masculine" style and was getting his tattoo on his wrist. This tattoo would create a permanent bond for all of us. Later my brother would return to get his, and my dad would eventually have his done. Six *Believe* tattoos in all. Six of us "willing" this child back to us.

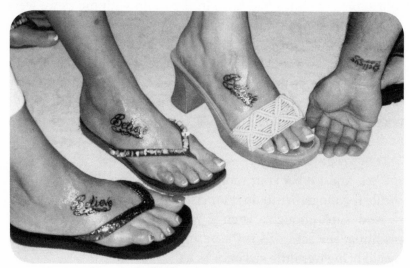

*Here are the first four fresh tattoos celebrating
our belief in Ashley's healing.*

Proudly, we returned to the hospital to continue our celebration of Ashley's birthday. When Ashley's little friends came to visit, we were saddened to see their confusion about why Ashley couldn't respond to them or play. I'll admit that I had pangs of jealously for the healthy, bouncing girls in my presence, while my daughter was battling her way back to us. I was smiling on the outside, but screaming on the inside.

Day 10
12:51 a.m.

Ashley's birthday

Even though we already celebrated with Ashley's Hannah Montana Birthday Party, today was a day we had planned to celebrate as a family. As much as we wanted to bring in a cake and have a little party at the hospital, we just couldn't bring ourselves to eat cake, knowing that Ashley can't ... and she loves birthday cake and ice cream. So we had balloons, and we sang "Happy Birthday" surrounded by Ashley's little sis and best friends Sydney and Ciera (by the light of a flashlight!). And the pile of presents is nicely arranged in the corner of the hospital room ... until Ashley can open them.

So in honor of Ashley today, her family did something that will be a daily, permanent reminder of how much we love this little girl and how much we believe in her. Tim, Mica, Grandma Sharon, and I got the word "Believe" as a tattoo. Uncle Mike has his scheduled to join the gang!

I can hear Ashley saying, "Daddy, I like your tattoo" or "Grandma, your tattoo is pretty." and boy, will she someday be surprised to understand the true symbolism behind them!

Ashley had a pretty good day ... she graduated to the 5th floor (room 503), which means she's no longer in the ICU. This is really good, as it's a lot quieter and she can rest more peacefully. (And we can too!) However, it is also scary because we don't know what is next from here or when. She has an MRI on Tuesday and we are hopeful that her brain is continuing to heal and with each day we'll see more progress.

So my advice I want to share with anyone who reads this is, please just cherish every moment you have with your kids and loved ones. When your son or daughter is riding their bike with a big proud grin, or swinging so high their toes are touching the sky, or giving you a hug or a goodnight kiss ... don't rush to the next thing on your list. Put down the Blackberry. Let the phone roll to voicemail. Take the moment in. Live it. Experience it. Cherish it. Because you never know if you'll get it back.

Love and Prayers,
Sondra, Tim, Ashley, Nicole

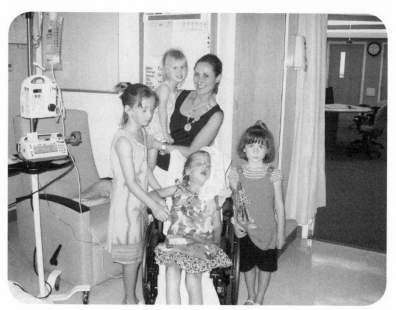

Ashley was not really awake much on her birthday, and I don't think realized it was her birthday, but she knew her friends and family were there to show their love.

Day 11
12:03 a.m.

Sunshine

Ashley had the joy of feeling sunshine on her face and the wind blowing her hair today! She is now free of all the IV lines and so we were able to put her in a wheelchair today and take her outside on the terrace. We sat outside for about an hour and she was very peaceful ... listening to some other children laugh and play.

We saw small improvements again today. Ashley seemed to enjoy her visit from physical therapy and worked on trying to regain control of holding her head up and moving her limbs. We saw subtle movements today that were not there yesterday. And at times it really felt that she was focusing and truly "looking" at us with very minor eye movements. She is vocalizing when she is upset and so we continue to try to understand her queues, but there are still no words.

One step, one day, one small accomplishment at a time. Ashley, sweet girl, our love for you cannot be measured by an hour, a day, a month, a year. There is no metric in this universe that captures the love we feel for you!! Keep up the hard work and we'll keep cheering you on!!

Love and Prayers,

Sondra, Tim, Ashley, Nicole

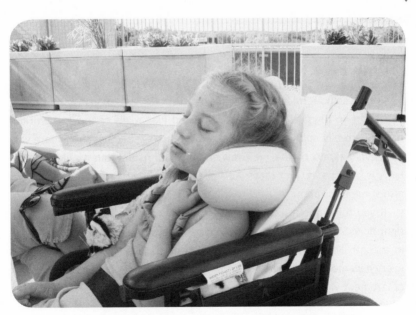

Taking Ashley outside the sterile hospital walls for a little sunshine and fresh air was such an amazing feeling. Her eyes remained closed but she seemed very calm.

We had enjoyed a few moments to sit outside with Ashley and breathe the pure, clean, outdoor air and just for a moment be "free" of the hospital environment. We had to learn to be grateful for these little things. In some ways we had been "awakened" to what was really important in our lives. And what wasn't.

The unspoken fears still remained. What if this was all there was going to be now for Ashley and for us? We didn't feel that she had fully returned to us, yet we didn't know what to expect. What if this is how our bubbly, active daughter is going to be now? Would she be confined to a wheelchair, unable to feed or bathe herself? What would it be like to care for her like this forever? We felt the guilt of thinking of others in these same circumstances and not wanting that to be us. We were afraid of losing what was and what might have been. Yet we were grateful that Ashley was alive.

Day 12
12:26 a.m.

Gratitude

We are so grateful for the amazing progress we have seen in Ashley today. She had two physical therapy sessions and was really trying and working hard. She really enjoys the sessions. I oftentimes think that she is here with us in every aspect of how we know and love our Ashley, but it's like her little body is frozen and can't react. At times you can see the determination, and also some frustration.

If you think about a new baby ... that's kind of the stage that Ashley is right now. She has to re-learn to hold her head, sit, use her hands and legs in a controlled fashion and eventually walk, talk, and eat again. So with every new movement, ever so slight, we see it, point to it, and feel the same amazement we felt the first time she did the things babies do that are such a big thrill!

So Ashley's big accomplishments today were holding her head by herself while the therapist counted to 100, pushing on an exercise ball, practicing sitting, moving her eyes to focus on people and objects, trying to talk! ... and smiling! Yes, I said smile! And yes, the therapists thought she was trying to speak. So they have recommended that we also begin speech therapy. I'll bet she's going to have a lot to say!

We are practicing mind-boggling patience. Even though it's "only" been 11 days, it feels like it's been a year! We are grateful for each small accomplishment that each new day brings.

Tonight we can say we are grateful for ...

-Ashley survived the operation and is here with us today
-she DID wake up from the coma
-her heart is stronger than ever before
-the seizures have not returned
-her chances of full recovery are highly optimistic
-our house didn't get blown away by the recent storm
-we have a beautiful, delightful, healthy 3-year-old daughter
-we have each other to lean on for strength and support
-we have the full support of an amazing network of family and friends
-we have understanding, supportive bosses
-we have the best health care expertise and care right here in Omaha
-and someone keeps mowing our lawn for us. Thank you for that!

Thank you to all of you for your continued support! It means so much to us! And thank you, God, for continuing to have your angels guide Ashley along her journey. We sometimes still hear the sink faucet running on its own, even though we are now in a different room. The angels are still here, they're just not crowding the room quite as much as before!

Love and Prayers,
Sondra, Tim, Ashley, Nicole

We had taken some liberties to decorate Ashley's hospital room. We hung a "Believe" painting above her bed and pictures on the walls and the windows. We made collages of our favorite family photos and hung them everywhere. Her friends and neighbors made huge "get well" posters that we hung in her room.

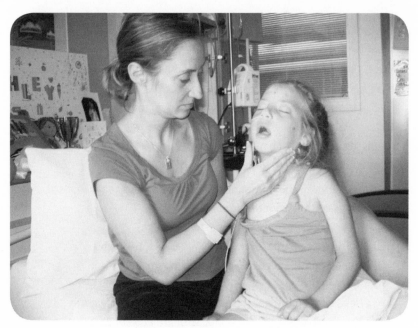

We patiently worked with Ashley to help her regain control of her head and her ability to sit up.

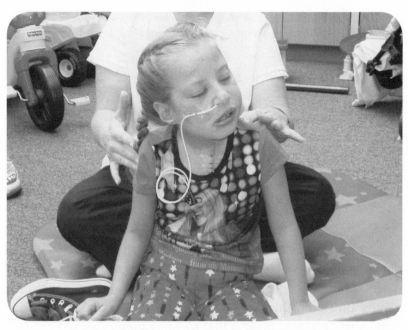

Therapy was challenging for Ashley as she was still sleepy and very weak. It was necessary to challenge her in order to begin the healing processes of her brain.

Ashley loved having her little sister in bed with her to snuggle.

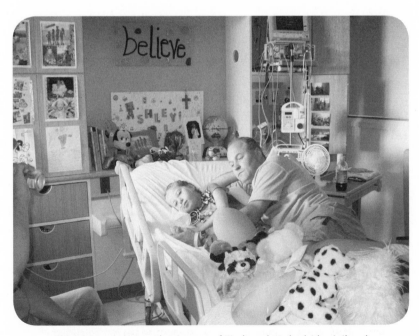

*This picture captures the essence of Tim's and my bedside vigil and
the love and caring we were pouring into Ashley.*

We brought in her favorite toys, books, stuffed animals, and soft, fuzzy blankies that smelled like home instead of the hospital. We played uplifting music constantly. We created our own little sanctuary! We were in our own little protective bubble.

Now that most of the tubes and wires were removed from Ashley, we took turns crawling into bed just to snuggle with her. It had become a routine now for Nicole to join us at the hospital in the evenings and on the weekends. She would lie in bed with Ashley and they would hold hands. Just having her little sister nearby seemed to be calming to Ashley and would later prove to be instrumental in her rehabilitation.

Day 13
8:12 p.m.

Steady as she goes

We are seeing our Ashley return to us little bits at a time! Today, I felt a wonderful, amazing, strong one-armed hug from our baby girl! We have seen more smiles and laughs and silly grins! And we think she tried to say "Love you"!

Ashley is participating in physical/occupational therapy twice a day now. She is making amazing progress in just three days. She is practicing rolling over from side to side, sitting, holding herself up, and head and neck control. And she had fun working out on a fun swing with the therapist! She is working SOOO hard! We are so proud of her.

We began to have some discussion today about a move to an in-patient rehab hospital. We are considering a facility in Lincoln, Nebraska, called Madonna, as they have a specialized pediatric rehab focus. Lincoln is about 50 miles from our house. When the caseworker asked where we would want to go for rehab, Tim's response was "wherever is the best"!! Ashley, your daddy is always looking out for you! Only the best for his little girl!

We probably won't be moving on to rehab until after the 4th of July holiday. And we are working with the neurologist to get her seizure medicine regulated. Tomorrow she'll have another EEG to check for any sub-clinical seizure activity. Probably won't do another MRI next week.

Today, Ashley had a special visit from her Aunt Mary who helped us pick the rest of the "goop" out of Ashley's hair from the EEG probes and gave her a spa-style hair washing, and a nice new set of braids! And now Tim and I get a special treat tonight ... an evening at home, while Aunt Mary stays with Ashley at the hospital! I think a glass of wine sounds good tonight!

All we can continue to pray and hope for is steady progress every day. We love you sweet girl!

Love and Prayers,
Sondra, Tim, Ashley, and Nicole

As Ashley's brain was "waking up" many interesting behaviors were presenting themselves. She wasn't able to control much of her body at all. There was constant drooling and teeth grinding. I remember the teeth grinding being so bad that it was almost impossible to sleep in the room with her. I began to worry that she would grind her teeth down to nothing.

Then there was the anguish we experienced with the uncontrollable "fits." Ashley began to have frequent episodes in which she would flail about and cry and scream. It was very disturbing because we would try to offer comfort, but the more we touched her, the worse it would become. It was as though her body was fighting to regain control.

Day 14
11:45 p.m.

Dreams

Do you BELIEVE that DREAMS can come true? I BELIEVE! Tim had a dream last night that Ashley stood up and asked for a drink of water! Well if I were her, I would want a drink of water too! And if you saw her rolling around in her bed like a little wiggle worm like she was doing tonight, you'd BELIEVE like I do that his dream will soon come true.

Wow! The power of all those positive, encouraging words must really be working as it's even coming through in our dreams now! That's an incredible transition, considering that this journey started out as "our worst nightmare" as was stated by Ashley's surgeon when we learned of the complications during her surgery. It has been our worst nightmare, as I'm sure any situation like this would be for any parent. Our children are so precious, that when a situation like this happens, it just zaps the life out of you. Literally. Nothing else matters!

Fortunately, the nightmare is over and our dreams for a wonderful future for our lovely little girl have returned.

Ashley had a very busy day! After a little woman-to-girl chat and a sleep-over with her Aunt Mary last night (I did get that glass of wine last night!!), Ashley had a heart echo and an EEG today. We are not expecting any concerns on the heart echo and still waiting for news from the neurologist on the EEG. She had another "salon treatment" to get the EEG glue out of her hair, a 1-hour physical therapy session (with a special cheering section including BFFs Sydney and Ciera), a visit from our pastor, a visit from our family doctor, a visit from one of Ashley's favorite teachers, and a visit from a representative from Madonna rehab! Whew! She should sleep well tonight. I hope so since I'm on night duty!

We are anticipating that we will probably move Ashley to Madonna Rehabilitation sometime early next week. The representative from Madonna was a very nice lady. She was very confident and reassuring that the therapists will be able to help Ashley recover. The first 3 days of Ashley's stay there will be spent with medical and therapist assessments and setting up her daily routine.

By the 3rd day, she said the team will be able to give a pretty good "estimate" for how long Ashley will need to be there. And then we'll go from there and extend her time as necessary as long as she continues to make progress. The facility looks very nice, and there is family housing, and we can also stay in the room with Ashley. They strongly encourage family and friends to participate in the therapy. We warned her that Ashley has a rather large fan club to cheer her on!!

And hats off to the rehabilitation team for getting Ashley started on her road to recovery. It is absolutely amazing to watch how they work with her and what a difference it is making already.

Sweet dreams tonight everybody!

Love and Prayers,
Sondra, Tim, Ashley, Nicole

Tim's dream was just one sign of how much we both longed for Ashley to return to us. We continued our daily vigil of hope and prayer and continued to draw inspiration from the constant flow of messages on the online journal.

What wonderful news! Little Ashley is going to be just fine! She is the miracle that will inspire others! Right now the gains seem slow but they will start to snowball. Soon this will all be a grand story of a wonderful miracle! The miracle that Ashley beat all the odds! Remember when I told you that Ashley would be ready to enjoy the fireworks on the 4th! She will be smiling and pointing! It will be a wonderful day of celebration! And next year she will be running around dancing with a sparkler! Sondra & Tim thank you so much for sharing your faith with us all! Your strength as a family and your trust in God is inspiring! Ashley is not the only one in the family that is drawing people to God! I think the Dubas family is AMAZING!! Still praying!

Our "Expect a Miracle" Friend

Ashley, I just wanted you to know that after the last week and a half I understand what true strength and perseverance are all about! You are definitely an inspiration! How can I or anyone close to you ever possibly consider giving up after seeing you fight so hard!? I can't tell you how INCREDIBLE it felt to see you roll over on your own last night and to see you almost completely sit up all by yourself!! Keep up the hard work baby girl! Please continue to amaze us?! I truly BELIEVE you're on your way back to us!

Next Tuesday I'll be getting "our" tattoo just like Mommy, Daddy, Grandma and Mica. Can't wait to show you. It's gonna be on my left arm, right next to my heart! See ya tonight after work. Love ya!

Uncle Mike

I work with your mommy and have read all about your surgery and each day after the surgery. Your mom is a wonderful writer!! My girls (age 12 and 9) have been reading with me. We have all been sending lots of prayers for you, your family and all the wonderful people that help you each day and are so excited to hear about your great progress!! Continue to keep pushing each day as lots of people from all over the United States are cheering for you. We continue to send our prayers from Nashville, TN.

Sondra's business colleague

Day 15
1:23 a.m.

Big girl panties

Ashley had a great day today! So on a lighter note I thought I would share a couple of my favorite quotes! My closest friends know that my "quote to live by" is "Put Your Big Girl Panties On and Deal with It!" Kind of my life motto! This quote seemed appropriate today, and I found another one that reminded me of Ashley.

Yeah, I'm a Big Girl
When I need to ... I can rise to any occasion.
I put on my "I-can-do-anything face,"
Jump in over my head,
and learn to swim on the way up.
but don't be fooled.
I struggle just as bad as anyone.

Underneath my "can-do" façade I'm shaking in my boots.
So if I get a little testy with you,
Don't take it personally ...
And don't tell me to
Put on my big-girl panties and deal with it.
I am wearing 'em ... but they're starting to bunch, OK!

You would understand why I thought of this quote if you would have seen the determination on this sweet little girl's face today. After all she has been through (it's been 2 weeks as of today), this little child continues to tackle every challenge we present to her and continues to rise to the occasion with grace. Ashley's middle name is Grace! And, we saw a bit of her ornery side coming out today (which she gets from her dad, although he may disagree!). This is actually wonderful because it shows that above the determination, strength and endurance, we are seeing that warm, sweet, silly personality re-emerge!

Today, Ashley's major accomplishments were no drooling, no grinding, and no coughing. These may seem like minor details (and perhaps more than you care to know about). However, these are common side effects of the drugs and the brain injury. Now that Ashley has been able to get these issues under control, she will be evaluated tomorrow to determine if she can begin eating! This is a huge step toward getting rid of the feeding tube which is currently supplying Ashley with all her nutritional needs.

Ashley had two really great physical therapy appointments today. It's been fun cheering her on! She got to take a visit outdoors, and a special "rock star" performance from a local guitarist and singer. He played his guitar and sang to Ashley. When he began playing his guitar, her eyes opened wide and lit up! It was beautiful to watch her response. Hopefully, she won't remember that he didn't know any Hannah Montana songs!

Tim is staying with Ashley tonight. And tomorrow we'll spend the 4th of July at the hospital as a family. This certainly was not our original plan, but what really matters the most is that we'll be together!

Love and Prayers,

Sondra, Tim, Ashley, Nicole

Day 16
10:31 p.m.

Happy 4th of July

Parades, sparklers, ice cream cones, firecrackers. That's how I always remember the 4th of July as a kid. So I am feeling sad today that Ashley is in the hospital. My anticipation of summertime and the 4th of July is a whole different kind of anticipation now. It's all about Ashley's recovery and not the typical summertime activities. However, I am reminded that today is only one day and it's only one 4th of July ... Ashley will have many more to celebrate in grand style.

The hospital was kind of quiet today so we took a stroll to the lobby and I dipped Ashley's toes in the little waterfall that runs through the lobby. I thought she would find it interesting. She didn't like it all that well, and protested! So we went for a ride up and down the skywalk and she thought it was fun to have Mom run down the sloped walkway pretending it was a hill! It would not have been so funny had I fallen down like a fool! Ashley seemed very agitated today ... maybe she does know that it's a holiday?

Her biggest treat today was ... are you ready for this ... CHOCOLATE PUDDING! What a treat! The therapists came in to do an eating assessment and so this was the first food they had her try. She took 3-4 bites and smacked her lips and opened when asked to open her mouth! So on Monday or Tuesday they are going to do some additional assessment to make sure she is swallowing and it's going down properly before feeding her more.

Grandma Sharon is staying with Ashley tonight. And we are spending the evening with Nicole watching the neighborhood fireworks. Doesn't seem the same that Ashley is not with us. But it's good for Nicole to spend some time with us, and she loves playing with the neighborhood kids as much as Ashley does.

Happy 4th of July everyone! I hope that you are spending it with your families and friends and cherishing every moment!

Love and Prayers,
Sondra, Tim, Ashley, Nicole

Day 17
11:50 p.m.

Rebirth

Today Ashley seemed more agitated. Happy one moment, upset the next. It was kind of an exhausting day, as she required a lot of attention trying to figure out what stimulus to remove or what to do to interest her and help her calm herself. She seemed downright "mad" during her physical therapy session today!

It occurred to me today that it's kind of like Ashley's been reborn. She has to retrace all the patterns and areas of key learning. Her agitation today, at times, felt like that of an infant who is not able to express their feelings through verbal communication, and therefore becomes frustrated and just has to cry to vent it out. This can be stressful with an infant, but seems even more so with a 7-year-old child flailing her arms and legs ... and can kind of hurt too! That little girl is getting her strength back for sure!

On the positive side, the teeth grinding and drooling has stopped, and it seems that some of her frustration is manifesting itself differently now. No one has confirmed this, but my opinion is that some of what she's experiencing is still side effects from the coma-inducing drugs (basically barbiturates) and her brain healing and the nerve endings all waking up again! And I think she's frustrated that her body doesn't yet react to what her brain may be trying to tell it to do.

We noticed today that while listening to her recent dance recital music ("Gee Whiz I'm in Showbiz"), she seemed to be dancing while lying in bed. She was moving her arms and legs as if to mimic the dance routine! It was a positive sign that her motivation is there, and the music definitely reaches her.

Nonetheless, it is daunting to think of all the things she must learn to do again—eating, talking, walking, going to the bathroom, spelling & reading, math, dancing—and just being a little girl!

So we just keep showering her with love and prayers, and she keeps teaching us something new every day. We love seeing the messages of encouragement, so please keep them coming. It helps us feel that we are not alone.

Love and Prayers,
Sondra, Tim, Ashley, Nicole

Day 18
12:20 a.m.

Friends are like stars

I saw a really neat quote recently, and it stuck with me:

"Friends are like stars. You may not always see them, but they are always there."

We are so overwhelmed by the support and encouragement from everyone. I am just amazed at the support we have received from people we have never even met. It warms my heart to know there are so many kind and hopeful people in this world. And that you are all cheering for this one beautiful little girl.

I have had people say, "Ashley is so lucky to have you as parents." But in all honesty, we are the lucky ones. I knew, without any doubt, from the moment she was born and we learned of her heart defect that she was a special gift from God and that we were "chosen" to be her parents for a special reason. Perhaps God knew that Tim and I could handle the journey that lay ahead. And we are truly blessed to have Ashley and to be connecting with all the wonderful people that are coming into our lives because of her.

Today was a challenging day for us and Ashley. She continued to have the uncontrollable "fits" of anxiety and frustration today. We spoke with several of the doctors and nobody can tell us exactly what is going on other than it's the process of her brain healing and her trying to gain control over the emotional center of her brain. So when these spells come on, we try our best to calm her and just ride them out.

We actually saw her more awake and very happy at times today. I know she's a girl and "mood swings" are to be expected, but she's much too young for that yet! So perhaps she's getting out the frustration, clearing out the cobwebs so to speak, so that her body can fully awaken. We would drive ourselves crazy trying to over-analyze any of the healing process she is going through. And so we are hopeful that we will be able to tap into some expertise once we move to the Madonna Rehab Center.

We are supposed to meet with the neurologist tomorrow, who will give the final okay for Ashley to move to Madonna. She could be moving as early as tomorrow or the next day. We'll let everyone know the plan as soon as it's established.

I've posted a very special photo of Ashley and Nicole "snuggling" and holding hands in Ashley's hospital bed. Ashley was very much aware that her little sis was there and she was reaching for her. It was very heart-warming to see.

Love and Prayers,
Sondra, Tim, Ashley, Nicole

Day 19
12:47 a.m.

Daddy's girl

The bond that has formed between Ashley and Tim will forever be strong. Tim was by her side last night and all day today, again protecting her, being her advocate, and making sure that the doctors and medical staff are on top of her care!

When he learned that the swallow test was not scheduled until Tuesday at 2, he raised a concern! When we weren't getting a visit from neurology, he continued to ask and have them paged, and it went on from there as we both expressed our readiness to expedite Ashley's final round of tests so we could move forward with rehab. And it worked!

The swallow test happened today and was successful. So Ashley can begin "practicing" with real food tomorrow! More chocolate pudding! And it's a good thing, because she pulled her feeding tube out twice today. A sure sign she is ready to be done with that nasty thing!

And neurology gave the green light, so tomorrow we go to Madonna in Lincoln! The Madonna folks were here to visit again today. We had a lot of questions for them about the recent anger fits that Ashley has continued to have. They reassured us that very strange behaviors often present themselves when the brain is healing. So, again, we feel happy to be taking this next step and think it will expedite Ashley's recovery immensely.

We hope to be released in the morning, and Tim and I will drive Ashley to Lincoln. The physical therapists are lending us a special car seat that will safely restrain Ashley for the drive. I am expecting that we'll make a quick pit-stop at home to pick up overnight bags and let Benny, the family dog, give Ashley some "kisses." He has been missing her! I overheard her talking to him a couple days before surgery and telling him, "I'll be gone for a while, but I will be back." It was almost as if she knew what was going to happen. And I trust that she knows she's coming back to us in time!

We'll let you all know how the transition to Madonna goes tomorrow!

Love and Prayers,

Sondra, Tim, Ashley, Nicole

Life Lesson: Life Is a Journey—Enjoy the Journey and Stop Thinking about the Destination

I have learned this from my children more than anyone. Children have active imaginations. They can create their own little make-believe world and step right into it, playing for hours without a care for the time ticking by on the clock.

As adults, how much do we "someday" our lives away once we've lost that innocence of childhood. We spend our time thinking about the things we'll do, places we'll go, people we'll visit, money we'll have, and happiness we'll discover "someday." The sad thing is that "someday" never comes.

We learned that when tragedy strikes, you're forced to just slow down and stop thinking about "someday" and focus on the journey that's right in front of you. You focus on one day at a time. And in doing so, there can be a sense of peace.

Coping Strategies: Mind Your Thoughts (Think Positive Thoughts and Focus on Positive Energy)

Many of the strategies we adopted were designed to cope with the fear that presented itself in the form of negative thoughts.

What-ifs. You need to eliminate the what-if thinking. In our case, it was, "What if she doesn't wake up? What if the brainwaves don't come back? What if she never talks? What if she never walks? What if she is disabled and in a wheelchair the rest of her life? What if?

The "what-ifs" will drive you crazy. It's easy for your mind to spiral into this type of thinking. Just let go of that. Focus on the moment. Focus on the next minute, hour, or day. Just focus on the furthest out you can see without the "what-ifs" entering the picture. Exchange those negative thoughts for positive ones. What if she heals and everything is just fine? Rearrange those possibilities in your mind.

In our case, it became what if everything turns out just fine? What are we going to learn from this? What are we going to change in our lives? How can we embrace this event and grow because of it?

Projecting positive thoughts was our strategy for displacing fear.

" **Every blade of grass has an angel that bends over it and whispers, "Grow! Grow!"** "

— Talmud

part two

Learning Everything All Over Again

" He who has hope has everything. **"**

— Arabian Proverb

" Each day comes bearing its own gifts. Untie the ribbons. **"**

— Ruth Ann Schabaket

Chapter Five

The Road to Rehabilitation

We were excited to be moving on to the next step of getting our daughter back. However, the thought of having Ashley at a rehabilitation hospital was hard to accept. For some reason, I think I had a negative perception of what I thought a rehabilitation hospital represented. I guess I thought it was a place for hopeless cases—for people who couldn't take care of themselves at home, but didn't need to be in the hospital anymore. All of our experiences with Ashley had been at the hospital.

This would be a new adventure. I really wished we could just be going home, but at this point, Ashley was in a wheelchair and had just learned to hold her head up and sit on her own. She had a long way to go to regain all that she had lost.

One of the things that was still troubling me the most was that she wasn't speaking yet. She was now alert and awake, but only utterances had been heard. I longed to be able to hear her voice and have her talk to us.

Day 20
3:50 p.m.

On the road to rehab!

We just got everything cleared and we are getting ready to leave the hospital for Madonna in Lincoln. Ashley has not wanted to get out of her wheelchair all day! She knows we are leaving. We'll make a quick stop home and then we'll be on our way. I'll send out an update later when we are settled.

Love and Prayers!
Sondra, Tim, Ashley, Nicole

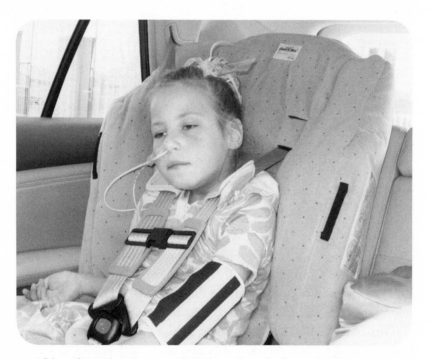

I felt as if I was bringing a new baby home from the hospital. Ashley sat in a specially designed car seat to keep her secure. Her arm splint was in place to keep her from pulling out the feeding tube that runs through her nose.

When we left the pediatric hospital, it had been the first time we were on our own outside of medical care for two weeks. I just wanted to snuggle with my sweet girl and be home, but that wasn't possible. The short visit home was bitter sweet.

*Tim helped Ashley sit on the floor and pet her dog, Benny. When
she felt his soft fur and wet kisses, her face lit up with smiles.
How desperately we wanted to keep her home.*

Day 20 continued
11:43 p.m.

On the road to rehab

Ashley waited patiently all day today to be released from the pediatric
hospital. Without a doubt, she knew it was time to leave. She didn't want to
lie in her bed at all ... she pretty much sat up in her wheelchair all day! She
had a really good therapy session and practiced "standing"!! We sang "Gee
Whiz, I'm in Showbiz" while she stood. I swear she wanted to dance!! And
then she got to eat yogurt as her practice session for eating, and did a great
job at that.

Last night was a little rough, as she pulled her feeding tube out twice ...
and it's not a nice process to put it back. So today we put a little Velcro arm

guard on her left arm which prevents her from reaching her nose and pulling the tube. Sounds mean, but it's better than the alternative! And she did ok with it.

Ashley enjoyed the ride in the car. We jammed to one of her favorite pop artists! It was very nice to stop in at home with her for a while. She loved seeing Benny, the family dog. He has really missed her and he showered her with sloppy kisses! She smiled and didn't mind! It was a joyous moment, but also kind of sad because I really wanted for us to be able to just stay home. But our journey is not over yet ...

We are all settled in at Madonna Rehab Center in Lincoln. We arrived this evening at about 6 p.m. and they were under a tornado warning! What's up with the tornados in Nebraska lately! This evening was spent getting Ashley settled into her room. It seems like a nice, quiet place. Her room has a "tree house" theme. I told her it will remind her of our family weekend stay in a cabin at Mahoney State Park last fall. Makes it feel like we are on vacation! (I only wish that were the case!)

Tomorrow, she starts at 7 a.m. with visits from all the therapists. We are happy to finally be here and it sounds like tomorrow will be a busy day. It kind of feels like it's the night before a big presentation or test or interview ... anticipation and high expectations and unfamiliar territory! Never in a million years would I have thought that I'd be bringing my 7-year-old daughter to a rehabilitation center. We are putting our trust and faith in God and the wonderful people we have heard about from Madonna.

When we arrived in Ashley's room, there was a brochure and an awesome quote:

> *Start by doing what's necessary; then do what's possible;*
> *and suddenly you are doing the impossible.*
> — *St. Francis of Assisi*

Please keep up the cheering for our girl. She has a lot of hard work ahead of her!!

Love and Prayers,
Sondra, Tim, Ashley, Nicole

Arriving at Madonna in the evening in the midst of a tornado was not what we had expected. But then nothing about this journey had been expected. As we drove there watching a tornado swirl across the cornfields, it seemed to be symbolic of this whole journey. Tornados are unpredictable; you don't know when they will strike land and how much damage they will do. This seemed to describe Ashley's brain trauma perfectly.

I felt an overwhelming sadness the night we checked Ashley into the rehabilitation hospital. It just didn't feel like we belonged there. Yet I was hopeful and desperate for these people to "fix" her. I wish I could say that we never ever had doubts about Ashley's recovery, but contrary to my postings in the online journal, the truth is we were constantly fighting the fears and doubts of what the outcome would be.

That day was also the eve of my fortieth birthday. For the past year I had been anticipating my birthday bash. It had been all about me. Me. Me. Me. I had bought a dress and shoes. I had been working out with a personal trainer and getting in shape. Honestly, I was obsessed with looking and feeling my best on my fortieth. I was going to host a party with martinis and sushi and celebrate "me"! Tim and I had even argued about why I needed to have this party.

And at that moment in time as I tucked my daughter into bed at a rehabilitation hospital, I realized how utterly selfish and ridiculous it had been for me to be so self-absorbed about a birthday. The reality struck me that all I wanted at this moment in time was for my daughter to be healed. I now had a completely new perspective on what truly was important.

Tim and I had decided we should both spend the night with Ashley. We were in such a state of uncertainty. Not knowing what to expect, we just both wanted to stay with her. The room was large, but didn't have much for "guest accommodations." We settled in with me sleeping on a vinyl sofa again. And Tim was sleeping in a reclining chair.

This would become our home away from home. Ashley would stay here and continue her healing journey. Tim, Grandma Sharon, and I would continue our rotation of trading places between home and Madonna. One of us was taking care of Nicole and the other Ashley. Neither Tim nor I had returned to work. Our focus was 100 percent on Ashley's recovery and getting our family back together.

Day 21
9:02 p.m.

A new chapter

Today Ashley officially started her rehabilitation, so it's now a new chapter in her story. She had a very busy day starting at 7 a.m. with assessments from all the therapists. As I was reflecting on all the new members of her "team" we met today I remember meeting Physical Therapist, Occupational Therapist, Speech Therapist, Physiatrist, Pediatrician, Case Worker, Social Worker, Chaplain, and many others! Wow!

Tomorrow morning her team will meet and discuss their assessments from today's observations and then provide their recommendations on appropriate goals and estimated length of stay. So we'll be anxious to hear their care plan tomorrow. Everyone has been very kind, caring, and sensitive to Ashley, and they seem to be very optimistic about her recovery. We also were reassured that much of the behavior we've seen is part of healing and not long-lasting.

We toured Madonna and realized it is a much larger facility than we could tell last evening when we checked in. Ashley enjoyed strolling in her wheelchair when we weren't in her therapy sessions. There's a good cafe with a lot of choices, some outdoor seating areas, and a beautiful chapel that has the most peaceful, quiet feeling. We took Ashley in there and said our "bedtime prayers," praying for all our friends and family and Ashley's recovery.

A few interesting stats about Madonna's Children's Rehab Program in 2008:

- Served thirty-five inpatients under 18 yrs old in 2007
- 17% were under 7 yrs old
- 54% were children with brain injuries
- 80% were discharged after an average length of stay of 18 days
- 93% of patients/families rated overall experience as excellent/good

Overall Madonna served over 2,171 rehab patients in 2007. And overall, Madonna served a significantly higher number of patients with traumatic brain injuries (70%) than the national (55%) or regional (51%) averages. So I think we are in a good place for brain injury recovery.

Quotes painted on the wall outside Ashley's room:

Out of difficulties, grow miracles.
— Jean De La Bruyere

Oh, the places you shall go.
— Dr. Seuss

Love and Prayers,
Sondra, Tim, Ashley, Nicole

Day 22
10:37 p.m.

Optimism

As I reflected more last night on our move to Madonna, I realized that there was one single difference that stands out. Madonna is a place that has such a sense of "optimism." Through the course of the day, not once had we heard anyone say "we don't know" or "we hope for the best" or "how could this have happened." What we heard over and over was "Ashley, you are beautiful. We are happy you are here. We are going to work hard on helping you get better so you can go home." I did not once feel any hesitation or doubt!

And then we walked down this long hallway of beautifully framed portraits of former Madonna patients and their printed stories. These are the stories of inspiration I was searching for! And there was one that really caught my attention about a young lady from David City, NE (a town not far from where Tim and I grew up). She was in a terrible car accident right before her senior year and had severe head trauma. She was unable to walk or talk when she came to Madonna.

After many months of hard work, she made it to her High School Homecoming in time to be crowned Homecoming Queen. But the part of her story that really stuck with me was the part about her volunteering at Madonna and going on to school to become a therapist. I had this immediate vision of Ashley using her experience through all of this, and her special gifts of compassion, kindness, and caring to do something similarly great … helping others to change their lives! This story spoke to me very deeply.

Ashley has a lot of hard work ahead of her. The care plan her team assembled and shared with us today is projecting a 4-week in-patient program for her. This is only an estimate and could possibly be longer. And it is expected that she will need to continue with out-patient therapy once she leaves Madonna (which she should be able to do in Omaha).

So her goals for the next 4 weeks are to achieve the following:

-Sit on her own without assistance
-Play with toys on her own while sitting
-Sit in a chair to write or eat
-Walk 100 feet with minimal help
-Go up and down eight steps holding railing
-Eat by feeding herself
-Dress and bathe herself
-Communicate her needs, using some words

We feel these goals are going to be a lot of work for Ashley but we BELIEVE they are attainable and that she has the determination!

She is already showing us that she wants that feeding tube out as she pigged out today on MORE CHOCOLATE PUDDING and her favorite ICE CREAM!! Tomorrow, she'll get to have breakfast, and when she is eating 50% of three meals a day, she'll get to have the tube feedings stopped. I think when she gets to that point, she'll really excel! Unfortunately, we can't take the arm splint off her left arm for more than a split-second and she's grabbing for the tube. The upside is that with her left arm restricted, it's forcing her to use her right hand more ... she's pretty darn smart!

She's a busy little lady with a very full daily schedule of 2 speech/ eating therapy, 2 occupational (fine motor) therapy, and 3 physical therapy sessions per day. The therapists have also begun using some strategies to minimize her agitation, which they have termed "tactile defensiveness." It means that she is over-stimulated and her brain can't process everything so she gets agitated.

And the best part is that her dog, Benny, is welcome as a visitor!

Tonight, Tim and I are going home to spend a little time with Nicole. Grandma Sharon is staying with Ashley overnight and will attend her therapy sessions tomorrow. I'll go down for part of the day tomorrow. And hopefully we can take Nicole for a visit this weekend!

Thank you for your continued prayers!

Love and Prayers,
Sondra, Tim, Ashley, Nicole

Coping Strategies: Accept Help (Even If You Think You Don't Need It)

You, like the rest of us, become accustomed to dealing with daily life on your own, within the walls of your own household. You really have no idea what's happening behind closed doors. Most people present themselves as though their lives are all roses. The reality is that everyone has his or her own problems. But we don't want anyone to know that we are less than perfect.

When a tragic event occurs, those barriers come down. In our case, we allowed our situation to be exposed to the world via the online journal. Likewise, opening up to the offers of help were not easy in the beginning. You may tend to think you can handle things. And sometimes it's okay to accept that you can't handle it all.

Whether it's an offer to provide a meal, walk the dog, mow your lawn, or just sit with you and hold your hand, be willing to be open to the offers. And also be aware of what is truly helping you versus what might be creating more stress. People want to help and they mean well, but sometimes they honestly don't know what to do.

And most importantly, help yourself! What I mean by that is you have to take care of yourself. If you are dealing with a challenging life event, you need to stay healthy and rested or the stress will consume you mentally and physically. I remember experiencing this. And I couldn't be of any help to my child when I couldn't be in the room with her because I was sick.

Eventually Tim and I became attuned to the need for getting adequate rest. Sleeping on the vinyl couch in Ashley's hospital room did not qualify as proper rest! And it became rather apparent at times who was getting rest and who wasn't. The one who had just pulled off a "night shift" was often less tolerable, more irritable, and more emotional. And the one who had gotten a full night of rest at home was more rational and better able to cope with emotions and deal with the processing of data being received from the medical staff. We realized that we needed to be aware of this and in a respectful way help each other to recognize this.

Chapter Six

Regaining Independence

Ashley had gone from a state of complete dependence on breathing tubes, IV lines, feeding tubes, and wires to monitor every bodily function. And we, too, had felt very dependent on the medical professionals who were managing her care. As her parents, we wanted our child back. We wanted her to be free of all the medical interventions. And we wanted to be able to care for her. With each new step forward, it meant we had our hands full.

Ashley was unable to feed herself, use the bathroom, or do really anything for herself. However, we felt that with the care she was receiving we were beginning to get some answers and were becoming more confident that this was all just part of the healing process. The uncontrollable fits that she continued to have were one area that had been very hard to process. Now we had a strategy for helping her to overcome the over-stimulation that was causing the fits.

The process of "rough brushing" was something that initially was very difficult for us. In the beginning it took two of us to hold her down. She would thrash and scream while we held her down and "brushed" her arms and legs. We used a little plastic brush that was very soft so it didn't hurt her. It reminded me of the brush you use on a newborn's head. We would do ten long strokes on one arm, then the other, then each leg. This was followed by tugging and stretching each joint. After a short break we would repeat the process. Break. And do it again. And we did this multiple times a day.

At first, I dreaded having to do this process. I felt like we were torturing our little girl after she had been through so much already. But it didn't take long and she began to relax as we were completing this procedure. And it eventually became soothing.

We were amazed that this process worked! Somehow this sensation of brushing her arms and legs was actually helping Ashley's brain to reorganize its ability to process sensory input. The therapists explained it this way. Close your eyes and become aware of all the sensations your body is experiencing. The temperature of the room. The sound of the air conditioning system. Background noises. Smells. Your feet touching the floor.

Our brains are simultaneously processing all of these sensations and we don't even realize it. Because of Ashley's brain injury, her brain isn't able to process all of these sensations simultaneously yet. And that's why she's having these fits. The brushing technique was developed as a strategy to help with that. It seemed crazy, but it worked.

I believe that this was a key moment of trust for us with the therapy team. There were things that couldn't be explained by medical science, and there were strategies to "fix" the things we could not understand through therapy. We knew we were in the right place for our daughter to heal and rehabilitate.

Day 23
12:48 a.m.

Independence day every day!

There is a message on the marquee at the Madonna front entrance. It says: "We celebrate independence every day at Madonna."

Today was a celebration of independence for Ashley! She is now totally free of all tubes, wires, and other such medical paraphernalia. She coaxed her way out of the feeding tube. It was by accident really. After eating a rather large, yummy breakfast ... and perhaps getting her tummy more full than recently accustomed, she "lost her breakfast" (trying not to be too graphic), and in the process disrupted the feeding tube and had to have it removed.

Once again, Grandma and Daddy went to work to protect Ashley! Grandma Sharon called us to tell us what was going on, and Tim immediately demanded that the tube not be placed back in. After all, if the child is eating on her own, why not let her! And so it was! Ashley has to prove herself over the weekend by not losing weight and eating enough calories and fluid to satisfy the pediatrician.

So for now, she is free! And I'm pretty confident she'll work hard over the weekend eating as much ice cream, pudding, and yogurt we can force upon her. We will get to the nutritional content later after crossing this immediate hurdle. I tell you what, this little girl does not do ANYTHING the conventional way. She is always surprising us!

Ashley's therapy sessions went very well today. The physical therapist is continuing with some rather interesting techniques of "rough brushing" her legs and using weighted blankets to help her get in touch with her body and the over-stimulation issues. It seems to be working as her fits of frustration are happening less and she's able to calm herself more easily. And the therapist told us Ashley had a major breakthrough today going from a seated chair position to a standing position (with support). It's clear that her muscles are strong, and it's a matter of "re-wiring" her brain to read the signals.

Ashley worked very hard today (7 therapy sessions) and hopefully will sleep well for Grandma Sharon again tonight. Has anyone noticed that my mom is a pillar of strength? She is so amazing and has been there to help Ashley and Tim and me since the day Ashley was born. We appreciate and love having her as part of Ashley and our lives!

So after Grandma Sharon and Ashley's "sleep-over" tonight, Tim, Nicole, and I will go back to Lincoln tomorrow for the weekend. The weekend therapy schedule is less aggressive (with only 3 therapy sessions tomorrow), so Ashley will be able to have a few visitors this weekend. And get rested for another week of hard work.

Quotes of the day:

Where there is great LOVE, there will always be MIRACLES.
— Willa Cather

The greatest thing in the world is not so much where we stand as in
what direction we're moving.
— Oliver Wendell Holmes

Love and Prayers,
Sondra, Tim, Ashley, Nicole

Day 24
12:46 a.m.

It's only one day

Today, we have focused on helping Ashley cross another hurdle ... eating! She started the day out good, but hasn't had much of an appetite today and has thrown up a few times. We aren't sure if she's just overly sensitive to certain flavors and textures, or if she has a little tummy bug, or what. We are feeling the pressure that if we don't force her to eat/drink the Dr will require the feeding tube go back in. So we've been kind of stressing about this today. And Tim is determined to not let the tube go back in!

And then it occurred to me that "it's only one day," so if she doesn't feel like eating today, she'll eat tomorrow! After all, how many kids eat consistently from day-to-day? And then I remembered how we felt the day when Ashley came off the vent and we worried about whether she could maintain her oxygen level and cough frequent enough. So, again, I remember it's only one day, and the difference one day makes in the scheme of the 24-day journey we've experienced can be pretty monumental, given what Ashley's been through already.

Grandma Sharon went home today. Tim, Nicole and I all spent the afternoon with Ashley. Ashley and Nicole "snuggled" in Ashley's bed and watched SpongeBob! And Nicole got to meet one of Ashley's "teachers," the physical therapist. We've told Nicole that Ashley is at a special "school" to help her remember how to walk and talk so she can come home. We figured this was a better description of what "rehab" means than to tell her Ashley is at another hospital. She seems to have handled it pretty well.

Tonight, Tim is staying with Ashley. And Nicole and I are staying in Lincoln with friends, who were so kind to open their home for us to stay!

We'll let you all know how the ice cream–pudding–cream of wheat–Sprite diet is going tomorrow! Those are the items we know Ashley will eat, so we've decided to focus on those and not introduce any of the disgusting pureed hospital food!

Love and Prayers,
Sondra, Tim, Ashley, Nicole

We were making the most of the situation. We tried to spend time together as a family on the weekends. Nicole would join us and we'd hang out in Ashley's room. We'd take walks around the Madonna campus or outside, pushing Ashley around in her wheelchair. We met other families that were there with their children. All of us were dealing with different circumstances and reasons for being there. Yet one thing remained the same, we were searching for hope. We wanted our daughter to be healed, and we wanted to resume normal life. Whatever "normal" might look like when this was all over.

Traveling back and forth between cities from where we lived to where Ashley was staying was about an hour drive. We adjusted to traversing this road almost daily. Rotating so that either Tim or I or my mom was present with Ashley at all times. There was never a moment during her rehabilitation that a family member wasn't present with Ashley. It was just very important to us that Ashley always had family present with her. We never wanted her to feel alone. And I truly believe in my heart that surrounding her with our constant love healed Ashley.

There were times that I yearned to be with Nicole at home. Then there were times that I was at home and I yearned to be with Ashley. Most of all I yearned for us to all be in one place together. It was good to watch Ashley and Nicole spend time together. It was good to see them reconnect and attempt to play together. And it was good to see them snuggle and be together. I knew that Nicole missed her sister too.

Day 25
11:41 p.m.

Together

Today was a really GOOD DAY! We were all together as a family, and it felt really GOOD!

Ashley did a GREAT JOB eating today, thanks to her dad doing a fabulous job of coaxing her into eating cream of wheat, pudding, ice cream, Sprite, and even ... broccoli cheese soup! I know, not a tremendously varied, nutritious diet, but enough to satisfy the pediatrician. So hopefully, Ashley has cleared one more hurdle!

So, we spent the day TOGETHER as a family! Ashley and Nicole snuggled in Ashley's bed and watched *The Fox and the Hound II*, one of their favorite movies! We are not sure, at this point, what Ashley is able to see, as the area of her brain that was injured controls vision. She looked at the TV at times, but she definitely "listened" and recognized the voices and songs. One of the songs that Ashley and Nicole have always sung together from the movie goes "TOGETHER, TOGETHER, OOH, OOH, OOH!" It was the theme of the day!

And then the best part of the day was our birthday celebration with the Haynes family! Since Ashley couldn't have cake or ice cream on her birthday, we had ice cream cake today in honor of Ashley's and my birthdays! She ate a whole piece! I ate the rest of the cake (no not really)! And then Matt and the girls went for a stroll...they looked like a parade walking down the street with everyone wanting their turn at pushing Ashley's wheelchair!

I have been touched by the sweetness these three little girls have shown and how kind and caring they've been to their little friend, Ashley! They will provide a tremendous boost to her recovery!

Love and Prayers,
Sondra, Tim, Ashley, Nicole

*Ashley seemed more like herself when her sister and friends visited.
They hugged, laughed, and snuggled.*

Ashley enjoyed being outside and having birthday cake.

Day 26

8:46 p.m.

WHATEVER

We had a really good day, followed by a sad day. It was a sad day because it's Monday and we are all missing ASHLEY. The Ashley that runs around singing "Gee Whiz I'm in Showbiz," and "Hip and a Hip and a Hip, Hip, Hip," and tattles on her little sister, and tells her mom every single day, "Mom, you are pretty." The hugs and kisses are returning, so that's a positive sign. But Ashley hasn't spoken any words since we've been at Madonna.

There are days like today that it's hard to be patient. It's tough not to let the mind wonder what the outcome will be. So we just keep reminding ourselves to BELIEVE in Ashley's strength and our love and the healing power of God and all her angels.

Ashley had a favorite phrase, "Whatever," with a little attitude, "WhatEVer"! And so I found this scripture on a little plaque that I bought her a while back.

Whatever is true,

Whatever is noble,

Whatever is right,

Whatever is pure,

Whatever is admirable,

Whatever is honorable,

Think about these things.

Remember God is with you

Whatever,

Whenever,

Wherever,

Forever.

— Philippians 4:8

Ashley, sweet girl, we miss you, love you, and will wait forever for your return.

Love and Prayers,

Sondra, Tim, Ashley, Nicole

I felt I was still on an emotional roller coaster. At times there were moments of great sadness and loss. Then there were moments of great joy and happiness at the accomplishments Ashley was making. Yet at times I felt a great sense of peace. I knew that we were all just trying to stay strong and continue to deal with a situation that none of us could have ever prepared for.

There were days that I felt we were all coping pretty well with the situation, and then there were days that I just felt the weight of the world on my shoulders. We were human. Not super-human. Just human. A friend reminded me that it was okay to acknowledge that there were weak moments and to let those feelings show. Nobody expected us to be positive all the time.

Day 27

11:42 p.m.

Reflection

There is a picture that caught my attention today at the entrance of Madonna (never noticed it until today). It says:

"There are no short-cuts to any destination worth visiting."

So true. Seeing this statement and reading the encouraging messages today led me to reflect on the past 26 days. In 17 days, Ashley has gone from not being able to move her limbs, hold her head up or eat food to sitting, standing, and eating her favorite foods! She's now sitting up in bed, standing with some support, and turning pages in a book.

Thank you to so many of you for helping me to regain perspective on how far we've come. And I also recognize that it sometimes takes moments of weakness to achieve the moments of greatness!

Love and Prayers,

Sondra, Tim, Ashley, Nicole

Through this entire process, I felt that I was experiencing an "awakening." I continued to post daily messages about Ashley's progress. Many people commented that they wondered how I came up with what to write every day. It was never a struggle for words. I felt I was so in tune to the "little" things. Revelations in my thinking were occurring every day. I was taking time to "smell the roses," so to speak.

I was noticing the small things and celebrating the mundane. It really was part of the conditioning of our minds to stay focused on the positive and to continue to "will" our daughter back to us. I knew that regardless of the outcome, we were going to be changed forever by this experience. We would be changed as individuals and stronger as a family.

♥ ━━━━━━━━━━━━━━━━━━━━━━━━━━━━━━━━━━━━━

Day 28
11:45 p.m.

Unconditional love

Ashley had a really good day today. Good eating, good therapy sessions, very snuggly. And she had a couple extra special "helpers" in her therapy sessions this afternoon! Her sister, Nicole, and her dog, Benny! Her therapists were actually thrilled to incorporate them both into her therapy.

We were all very impressed with how Benny and Nicole both joined right in and it seemed very comfortable having them there to be part of Ashley's day. After all, they are such a big part of her world. It is so apparent the "unconditional love" she receives from her little sis and her best buddy, "Benny the Beast"! Benny lay on the floor in her room and was really a good dog all afternoon and evening.

And Nicole, I have to say, has adapted amazingly to the situation that we are all facing as a family. She is showing her strength as well. As much as she is probably confused about what's happened to her sister, whom she idolizes, she has never shown anything other than love, understanding, and kindness to Ashley since the first day she visited Ashley in the hospital with all the tubes running this way and that way.

The other day when we were feeding Ashley, Nicole was sitting in the corner saying, "Good job, Ashley!" "Keep eating like a big girl, Ashley!." And today, she thought it was cool to get to go for a spin around Madonna in Ashley's wheelchair.

Nicole is about to turn 3 in August and is a sweet little blonde-haired, blue-eyed girlie-girl! She likes to wear high heels, play dress-up, read Fancy Nancy books, play with dolls, and she has a tremendous imagination! I have to believe, that as much as we will all take away something special from this experience, and we all know that Ashley is destined for something great,

I believe that is true for Nicole as well. She is only 3, but her character is being molded and shaped by this experience, and I think it will teach her wonderful things about love, compassion, and kindness to others.

She and Ashley will always share a special bond, and it is wonderful to know that they will always be there for one another. Nicole, you are an amazing little girl, and we love you!

Thank goodness for Aunt Mary. She's really a gem! She's giving Tim and me a break and is staying with Ashley the next couple nights so that we can spend some time at home. We'll be anxious to hear what she sees firsthand of the progress Ashley has made, as we sometimes overlook the significance of her progress since we are there with her every day.

Love and Prayers,
Sondra, Tim, Ashley, Nicole

A special bond was developing between Ashley and Nicole. They spent a lot of time snuggling in Ashley's bed. Being able to bring Benny to visit was such a special moment for her and made our little hospital room feel more like home.

Day 29
12:16 a.m.

Time

What is time? We have spent a lot of "time" recently thinking about ... How much time will Ashley spend at Madonna? How long before she comes home? How long before she walks, talks? How long before our lives are back to "normal"? How long before we can resume our jobs and careers?

I almost had a "meltdown" today when I walked in the store and saw the back-to-school "extravaganza" display! Immediately I thought, "Oh my God. Ashley won't be going back to school on August 13th." And I thought how unfair it was that we wouldn't be doing the normal shopping for backpacks, notebooks, and crayons in keeping with the timetable the rest of her class will be following. And then I stopped myself, and remembered that time is all "relative." Ashley WILL go back to school in her own TIME.

So today, Tim and I took some TIME to have a break. Tend to some things at home. Move Nicole's "big girl bed" into her room (she was quite proud!). Go out to dinner/date night for the first time in over a month. And reflect on everything! It was good for us to take some time to renew our spirits and regain perspective on the situation we are facing. And in the meantime, Ashley had a great day with her Aunt Mary ... doing therapy, getting pampered, and learning to push the wheelchair buttons to open doors!

As I reflected on this notion of "time" today, I found some interesting quotes that I wanted to share:

There is never enough time to do everything, but there is always enough time to do the most important thing.
— Brian Tracy

Time is a companion that goes with us on a journey. It reminds us to cherish each moment, because it will never come again. What we leave behind is not as important as how we have lived.
— Captain Jean-Luc Picard

Events in our lives happen in a sequence in time, but in their significance to ourselves they find their own order; the continuous thread of revelation.
— Eudora Welty

Love and Prayers,
Sondra, Tim, Ashley, Nicole

Day 30
11:43 p.m.

Amazing grace

After being home for just a day and a half, we were breathless with amazement when we walked into Ashley's room at Madonna today! She was sitting so upright, strong, and graceful in her bed. And of all things ... playing her Hannah Montana guitar!

One of our pastors from our church had come for a visit and brought Ashley a beautiful pink prayer shawl that had been knitted by a group of 20 women from the church. It was a special gift sent with much love, and care, and prayer! We will cherish it for what it represents and the warmth that it brings.

Ashley looked at us, with the same familiar silly-girl smiles we remember. She looked like "herself" and seemed very "happy," the pastor commented. I just couldn't get over the noticeable difference in just a short period of time! Aunt Mary must have had a pretty serious "girl-talk" with Ashley while she was staying with her the past couple days.

So, I guess, I now understand what everyone else tells us they see as such amazing improvement. Being away for a couple days and regaining some perspective enabled us to see it as well.

Amazing Grace. Grace is Ashley's middle name! And she is conquering this challenge with truly Amazing Grace!

Love and Prayers,
Sondra, Tim, Ashley, Nicole

Day 31
11:23 p.m.

Butterflies

Many of you know that Ashley and I are both fond of butterflies. When Ashley went to preschool she selected a butterfly as her symbol, which was used for visual recognition of where to place her backpack, etc. I have always cherished the butterfly for its representation of "transformation." It goes through a process by which a caterpillar magically becomes a beautiful butterfly. It occurred to me today that Ashley is going through her own transformation to become a beautiful butterfly!

Nicole, Tim, and I did a fun little project today. We decorated little mesh butterflies with glitter glue and rhinestones. Tomorrow we will take them to Madonna to hang from the ceiling in Ashley's room! Something to catch her attention and bring her joy!

Ironically, I watched Nicole running around outside this evening chasing a little white butterfly. She giggled and smiled as she followed it flitting from shrub to shrub. I felt this sudden peace. It was a feeling that my eyes are wide open to the "signs," as if pieces of a puzzle are falling in place. I wondered, are there angel butterflies?

A couple weeks before Ashley's surgery, we had a little butterfly habitat. We sent for the larvae, which came in the mail (yuck!), watched them turn into cocoons, and eventually turn into butterflies. Then we released them outside and watched them fly free! The girls thought this process was really neat to watch. So tomorrow we will hold another "butterfly release" in Ashley's room at Madonna!

Ashley spent the day again today with Grandma Sharon. She only had a couple therapy sessions. Noodles—the wiener dog came all the way from Grandpa Dale and Grandma Sharon's farm for a visit. We listened to her laughing and squealing over the phone as Noodles jumped on her lap and smothered her with "kisses."

Ashley's had a good day. And I think it's been a good day for Grandma Sharon too ... as she said she's gotten lots of kisses and snuggles from our girl today!

Since you all know I like inspirational quotes, here are a couple butterfly quotes:

Happiness is as a butterfly which, when pursued, is always beyond our grasp, but which if you will sit down quietly, may alight upon you.
— Nathaniel Hawthorne

There is nothing in a caterpillar that tells you it's going to be a butterfly.
— Buckminster Fuller

Love and Prayers,
Sondra, Tim, Ashley, Nicole

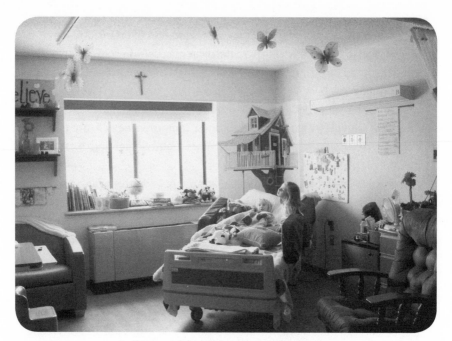

In the peacefulness of Ashley's hospital room
at Madonna, which we called the "Miracle Room."

Coping Strategies: Seek Sources of Inspiration

My friends discouraged me from typing the word *stroke* into Google. They feared that I might discover a lot of well-intended scientific data about outcomes that were less than positive. I knew that we needed to find sources of inspiration to plug the holes where the negative thoughts would seep into our minds.

We turned to uplifting music, books, quotes, medals, jewelry, photos, posters, and pocket charms. We went so far as to get permanent tattoos. The idea was to create an imprint that engaged the senses visually, or through sound or touch, so that we could stay connected and focused on the goals of our daughter's path to healing.

In the end, I believe that it was the key to our daughter's healing. All the positive energy and belief was what was breathing life into our fragile little girl and giving her the strength to fight for her life.

Chapter Seven

Hearing Her Voice Again

*I*t had been thirty-two days since our daughter had spoken to us. I have to say this was one of the most painful aspects for me of Ashley's rehabilitation process. Losing the gift of hearing your daughter's voice speak to you was heartbreaking. Not being able to receive any communication from her about what she was feeling and experiencing was hard to process as well.

Perhaps this affected me so much because Ashley's early medical challenges as a baby had also robbed her of her voice. The cooing that babies do seems like just gibberish, but in fact, it's integral to the development of speech. Since Ashley had a tracheotomy as a baby, she didn't even have sound for many months. With a breathing tube inserted at the base of her neck, the air wasn't allowed to travel past her vocal cords. Ashley would cry and there would be tears, but no noise.

This was very difficult to process at first. But we accepted that this is how it was and loved her all the more. Over time as her airways matured and we were able to adapt the breathing tubes, vocalization became possible. But it meant that she would have many years of speech therapy to help her develop her speech.

I think subconsciously I was recalling those early days when we longed to hear our baby's sweet voice. Oh, how precious those sounds were to us and the words that took so long to develop. Now Ashley was starting all over with that process again.

♥ ──

Day 32
12:26 a.m.

Rejoice!

Today was a VERY special day!! Ashley surprised us with actual words today! So here's the funny part ...her first word of the day: "Icky" (not sure if it's an actual word). Her second word: "abre," which is Spanish for "open" (learned from 7 years of watching Dora the Explorer cartoon), and her third word: "Mommy"!

These were not the utterances resembling words we have heard from her previously. These were very clear, precisely spoken words! She was so proud to have this breakthrough that she went on repeating *abre* over and over as if she were singing them and letting her voice be heard at last (smiling and laughing the whole time)! We absolutely could not believe what we were hearing!

Now I understand what the therapists have been telling us about some things just coming back suddenly and automatically! Grandma Sharon and Nicole were playing with a Dora book and saying "abre," and all of a sudden, Ashley just spit out the word *abre*!

Her other major accomplishment today ... she fed herself (holding with her left hand) a bean burrito and cinnamon chips from her favorite Mexican restaurant! What a treat to watch her! And then she later fed herself "crispies," a homemade pastry treat that her Grandma Marge brought today. Wow!

So I chose today to share a picture with everyone. It's a photo taken as Ashley was walking with her dance class to perform at her dance recital 5 days before heart surgery. Ashley is the last one walking behind her group, and she is silhouetted by a bright light shining through the window.

When I viewed the photos that evening, I had an ominous feeling when I saw this picture (I feared losing Ashley—that it was a bad omen). Again, when I came across this picture, as Ashley lay in a coma at the pediatric hospital, I felt disturbed and haunted by this photo.

Today, I have a new perspective on this photo. It has a happy feeling of rejoicing, as I now understand it was truly a sign that she is walking into the light of the grace of God and His angels, as they prepared her for her journey. It's amazing what our minds have the power to think!

This is the day the Lord hath made, let us rejoice and be glad in it!

Love and Prayers,

Sondra, Tim, Ashley, Nicole

Ashley was walking into the light. Only the circumstances we faced would have ever caused a mother to interpret this photo in the way that I did during my darkest moments. Shifting my perspective on the meaning of this photo was an amazing revelation.

Day 33

1:22 a.m.

Awakening!

I really don't even know how to put this into words! The day went something like this: Tim stayed with Ashley last night, and when I called this morning to check in with him, Ashley was saying, "Hi, Mom" and "I love you" on the phone!

"I Love You, I Love You, I Love You" ... as if she had to make up for all the days she couldn't say it! Of course I was overjoyed. About an hour later, Tim calls me and I listen to Ashley counting to 70! Again another call a couple hours later: Ashley singing "Happy Birthday," "Twinkle Little Star," "Row Your Boat," "Itsy Bitsy Spider"! The whole song—every word—just like she would have always sung them! And then ABC's and counting to 100 by 5's in sing-song rhythm!

We listened in awe and couldn't believe what we were hearing. It's as though Ashley has suddenly awakened! Or at least the area of her brain that is responsible for her speech has finally reconnected. If you have children and remember the joy of hearing the first word, multiply that by a million, a billion, a trillion! That's how elated we feel today!

Ironically, I've been reading a book that I found at the store (by "accident") called *My Stroke of Insight*. It's written by Jill Bolte Taylor, Ph.D., a brain scientist, who at the age of thirty-six suffered a massive stroke to the left hemisphere of her brain (the same side on which Ashley suffered the most damage). The book is her account of what it felt like to observe her mind deteriorate and lose communication with the external world, all the while still being alive and thinking inside her head. She lost her ability to talk, walk, read, or write, but after 8 years recovered 100%. This book has been a godsend, as it has really helped us relate to what Ashley must be experiencing, and it is very eloquently written, yet easy to grasp.

A particular excerpt from the book really helped me rationalize what I can only imagine Ashley has been experiencing these past few weeks "in silence."

Excerpt: Jill has called a colleague for help during her stroke (after it took 45 minutes for her to remember how to dial a phone number): "As he picked up the receiver, I could hear him speak, but my mind could not decipher his words. I thought, oh my gosh, he sounds like a golden retriever! I realized that my left hemisphere was so garbled that I could no longer understand speech. Yet, I was so relieved to be connected to another human being that I blurted out, 'This is Jill. I need help!' Well, at least that's what I tried to say. What exactly came out of my mouth was more akin to grunts and groans, but fortunately Steve recognized my voice. It was clear to him that I was in some sort of trouble ... I was shocked, however, when I did realize that

I could not speak intelligibly. Even though I could hear myself speak clearly within my mind, 'This is Jill. I need help!' the sounds coming out of my throat did not match the words in my brain … Although my left hemisphere could not decipher the meaning of the words he spoke, my right hemisphere interpreted the soft tones in his voice to mean that he would get me help."

This book has truly been "insightful" in understanding the magnificence of the mind and the incredible power it has.

When I spoke with Tim and with Ashley this evening, Ashley was "conversing" with me. It took her a while, and it was obviously frustrating for her, because she knew what she wanted to say but struggled to get the words out … "Mom, what time will you be coming?" I can't wait to get to Lincoln tomorrow to "talk" with Ashley!

All the prayers are being answered by God! Thanks to everyone for your continued support!

Love and Prayers,
Sondra, Tim, Ashley, Nicole

Absolute joy and happiness poured out of Ashley's mouth when she spoke those first words. You can see it clearly in her expression. And the joy and pride on Tim's face too.

Gee whiz

"Gee Whiz, I'm in Showbiz. Oh boy, what a joy. I'm right where I want to be. Just look at me!"

This is the first verse to Ashley's dance recital song. We have played this song over and over and over for the past 34 days. And I can sing this verse in my sleep (and I think that I have on several occasions). It's one of the key things that has calmed Ashley when she's been agitated. So we play it quite often. You would think I would be able to sing the entire song for as many times as I've heard it … but I can never remember the words beyond the first verse. Ashley sang the ENTIRE SONG beginning to end, followed by a little humming of the melody and a "cha-cha-cha"!

Ashley, take a bow! You deserve a huge round of applause! How much we have wanted to hear you sing this song again! How many times I have remembered in my head how much you enjoyed practicing this song! Next challenge … dancing to Gee Whiz! And I have no doubt, you will do it sweet girl!

Today, Tim said Ashley was a little more tired … lot that she accomplished yesterday. But when Nicole and I arrived today, she was calling us by name. She could say her birth date when asked. She remembers her best friends' names (Sydney and Ciera)! She knows the city and state in which she lives and her dog's name. Ashley is responding with "yes" and "no" when asked questions. And she said, "I like it," while eating her bean burrito tonight! It's clear that the cognitive connections with speech are still slow, but are definitely re-firing!

Love and Prayers,
Sondra, Tim, Ashley, Nicole

Day 35
10:20 p.m.

I want to go home

Ashley spent much of the day saying "hey dude," "bye dude," and "cherry nut ball dude." Madonna was a "dude ranch" today (I know ... a little goofy!). She was very active today in her repetition of familiar phrases and ABCs and counting to 100 by 5s! When we walked down the halls on our way to therapy, she was turning heads with her singing! And her affectionate side was showing today as she told all her therapists "I love you" instead of goodbye!

She finished phrases and words for me when I was reading her some of her favorite books. And she is initiating some cognitive communication when she wants or doesn't want something. For instance, she was telling her physical therapist "stop," when she had to work too hard. And twice today, out of the blue, she said, "I want to go home."

I think she has full awareness that she is not at home. She was constantly saying "mommy" as if she had something to tell me. But when I asked "what," she didn't have anything to say. So I think there is probably a lot on her mind that she just doesn't know how to communicate yet. It will keep coming. I asked her a couple questions today about whether she remembers her special heart day and our wish the day of surgery in the wishing well. She said "no," but seemed to be thinking a lot about what's happened and why she is here.

She was somewhat frustrated in physical therapy today, being pretty defensive to touch and not wanting her feet on the floor/standing. In discussing this with the therapists, our theory is that she's got a lot of new things she's trying to process all at once now that the speech is coming back. It's a lot of stimuli to process all at once.

She got to go to the "school" at Madonna today, and played "Go Fish" with some other girls. She was a little overwhelmed, but did participate and had the whole table laughing at her "hey dude" expressions! Friday she gets to do therapy in the pool, which she will really like!

Overall, we had a really great day! And the fact the Ashley now knows that she wants to "go home" will be the best motivation for her!

Love and Prayers,

Sondra, Tim, Ashley, Nicole

Living at Madonna with Ashley was a humbling experience. We had no privacy because we slept on the couch in her room. Nurses came in during the night multiple times to check her vital stats. Fortunately, there was a private bathroom, with a shower in her room. But somehow I never got used to showering there. I would rush through a shower, get dressed, and throw a pony tail in my hair so that I could be available to help Ashley if she woke up.

Sleeping at night had become a challenge, as Ashley had begun experiencing a very repetitive speech pattern. She would awake during the night and repeatedly call my name. "Mom. Mom. Mom. Mom." While I welcomed the fact that I could now hear her voice and she was communicating with me, it often made sleeping a significant challenge at night. And many times she needed help using the bathroom, which meant lifting her into a wheelchair and onto the toilet. Then holding her steady on the toilet and transferring her back. I loved that little girl and would do anything for her. However, she wasn't a baby. And so taking care of her needs was physically demanding.

Day 36
11:12 p.m.

Destinations

One of my favorite sayings is that in order to change your destination, you have to change directions. Or said another way, if you keep going in the same direction, you will always end at the same destination.

Ashley has clearly stated that her intended destination is HOME! She continued to state today that she wants to go home. And I think she was sad today when Mom, Dad, Nicole, and Mica left to go home and she had to stay. After we got home, Grandma Sharon called and said that Ashley wanted to talk with us. Amazingly, she had a pretty good phone conversation with us. She wanted to know what time we would be coming tomorrow and telling us she loves us! And that she gets to go to the pool tomorrow!

Today was a very busy day ... starting at 8 a.m. with continuous therapy. She is having a bit of a setback because of one of the side effects of her seizure-prevention medication. It causes elevated ammonia levels in the body (due to impact to the liver functions), which can cause drowsiness, irritability, and confusion. This kind of explains why she's been tired and defensive about standing and doing some of her therapy. This girl is trying to work hard so she can go home. The last thing she needs is the meds to be holding her up!

So the doctors are discussing a "change in direction" on the meds so that we can keep Ashley on track. So we'll see what the plan is tomorrow.

Love and Prayers,
Sondra, Tim, Ashley, Nicole

Day 37
11:28 p.m.

Swimtastic!

Ashley had a SWIMtastic day! She had her first pool therapy session and absolutely loved it! She got to sit in a chair and ride an "elevator" down into the water. The water was 92 degrees, so it felt like a nice big bathtub! When her legs hit the water and she started going into the water, her eyes lit up and she just laughed and laughed!

She kicked and blew bubbles and chased mom in the water (yes, I got to get in too)! She practiced standing and jumping, and seemed a little more willing to do these exercises in the water than what she has been on "land"! So we talked with the therapists about doing a lot more pool therapy sessions. However, we'll have to do them late in the day. It was about a 45-minute session, and she was really wiped out afterward. But she really enjoyed it.

Ashley had a few visitors today—one of the pastors from our church and our next-door neighbors. They were all amazed at the difference since they last saw her at the pediatric hospital. Ashley was more alert and talkative today. (I will tell you what. She's in the best mood whenever she's been hanging out with Grandma Sharon for a couple days!) Ashley and Nicole were so giggly today. Nicole stands on the foot-rests of Ashley's wheelchair and rides with her. And Ashley was giving Nicole kisses all day! They really miss being together. It's just so cute to watch them.

Ashley was initiating more conversation today instead of just repeating things we ask her to say. She's still calling everyone a "nut-ball-head" and a new one "ice cream-nut-ball-head"! She played "I-Spy" and "Simon Says" with Nicole and the speech therapist today, and actually participated by taking her turn at the games. And when we told her we were going "bye-bye" this evening (as I tried to avoid the use of the word "home"). She said, "Where are you going?" So I had to tell her that Dad, Nicole and I were going home and that Grandma would stay with her. And that we would be back tomorrow!

Love and Prayers,
Sondra, Tim, Ashley, Nicole

Day 38
11:06 p.m.

One more week

While Grandma Sharon was with Ashley today, Ashley sat up in bed and said, "Mom, Dad, Nicole, I've got one more week and then I'm coming home!" So it's apparent that Ashley's been listening and hearing EVERYTHING we've been discussing with her therapists, even when we sometimes think she's not listening.

Ashley's tentative discharge date is a little over a week away. And, yes, she has accomplished a tremendous amount since she's been at Madonna! Everyone here is very pleased with her progress. The one thing that may be reason for her to stay longer is that she has not been able to stand independently and begin walking. The physical therapist has no doubts that Ashley will be walking again. It just may be on a timetable that is slower than we would hope for.

So we'll have to weigh the benefits of having her at home (which is what she wants) to continue rehabilitation versus having her at Madonna where the rehab is very intense. Then, there's the fact that we will need to accommodate the wheelchair and transportation to/from therapy ... and carrying Ashley from her chair to bed, bathroom, car, etc. (She's eating so well, that she's gaining weight ... good for her! Not good for our backs.) So we've been encouraging her that she needs to work really hard this next week in her therapy sessions, especially with Miss Laura, her physical therapist, so that she can begin walking so she can go home!

Grandma Sharon was doing a lot of "practicing" standing with Ashley today, and she seemed to be responding quite well to her encouragement! I told my mom that she may have just earned herself a "live-in" physical therapist job!

I am staying with Ashley tonight. Tim and Nicole will come to Lincoln tomorrow, and we get to have an "outing." We are going to take Ashley to the park for a picnic. We got clearance on getting the wheelchair in the car and having her ride in the car seat that we had borrowed. And the Haynes family is planning to come join us. Ashley will LOVE seeing her friends and getting a chance to go somewhere. And this time, she'll be able to sing songs and laugh with them!

So, we'll encourage Ashley to work extra hard this week! And we'll pray extra hard that she'll make additional progress so she'll be able to come home soon!

Love and Prayers,
Sondra, Tim, Ashley, Nicole

Coping Strategies: Communication

It's a good idea to create a plan for how to stay in communication with family and friends. This might be something you plan ahead of time. And in other cases you may not have the opportunity to prepare, so it may be something you need to devise in the moment. In any case, it's common that there is a contingency of people who feel a need to become informed about your situation. That can put a lot of pressure on you to feel that you have to keep everybody informed.

Technology is a great tool for disseminating information. Tools that can be used easily from anywhere include online journals, blogs, Facebook, Twitter, and email lists. If you're not the type of person who engages with these technologies, you can always appoint a family member who can be that focal point for disbursing information.

These tools can also give you a common place to receive encouragement and support, when you are ready to receive it. For us, the online journal became a lifeline of encouragement, support, and prayers. There were times that I could literally visualize hundreds of people in the room with us praying, because that many people were interacting with Ashley's online journal site.

Use the tools and technologies in whatever way is comfortable to you. You don't have to feel as if you need to share everything. We were very transparent about sharing our raw emotions and feelings. Not everybody is comfortable with that. That's okay. Share what is comfortable that helps your family and friends stay connected and helps you in the ways that you most need the help.

Having a communication plan in place can also create space for you to deal with the situation at hand. I recommend, in the moment, that you shut off the cell phone, texting, and email. Slow down. Allow yourself to absorb what's happening and process it slowly. Stop the intrusion of people seeking you out and create a path of communication that is controlled based on your terms.

Chapter Eight

I Can Stand on My Own Two Feet

Day 39
12:11 a.m.

Picnic in the park!

Ashley had a break from therapies today, so she and I slept in and stayed in our PJ's until noon! What a treat! We snuggled and read books and Ashley said she wanted to watch TV. So we watched *Fox and the Hound II,* one of her favorites. It's still not apparent whether she is able to see (or whether her brain is able to interpret the messages of what she is seeing), but she knows the songs of the movie and so she still enjoyed it.

Friends came to visit with their brand new puppy today! Puppy breath and little giggling girls—two of life's simple pleasures! We took Ashley on her first real outing since before surgery. We drove over to Holmes Lake Park, sat on a blanket, watched the ducks, and played with the puppy!

Ashley lay back on the blanket and looked at the sky and said, "I'm pretending that I'm at the beach." It was a pretty hot/humid day in Nebraska today, so we went in the evening hoping it would be cooler. Unfortunately, Ashley was starting to get tired by then, so we kept the outing kind of short. I think she enjoyed getting out.

Of course we continued to hear today Ashley's ongoing request, "I want to go home." So tonight, I told her a motto to keep repeating to herself this week: "I can stand on my own two feet. I can stand on my own two feet. I can stand on my own two feet ... " Ashley, sweet girl, I have no doubt you will continue to WOW us! And I know that you can stand on your own two feet!

Love and Prayers,

Sondra, Tim, Ashley, Nicole

Ashley's vision had not healed yet. I think that is why she enjoyed touching faces to experience the people around her. She could feel the warmth of the sun on her face and recalled our many happy times at the beach.

Having a family outing along with our friends was such a wonderful, special experience. However, I also remember being very sad. Ashley was confined to a wheelchair while the other girls ran around and played and fed the ducks. Ashley was content to lie in the sun. But I couldn't help worrying about whether she would be able to resume her life playing with her friends. I guess those thoughts would have been worthy of a snap of my wristband to bring my thoughts back to a positive place.

Ashley was content being outside in the fresh air. As her mother, I struggled to see her sitting in a wheelchair while her friends ran around feeding the ducks.

Day 40
11:14 p.m.

Stand on your own two feet

We kept saying our motto today: "I can stand on my own two feet!" Ashley really wants to come home and so this is her motivator. Today she was being a really big girl for her daddy, trying to focus on getting up on those feet.

Tim spoke with the caseworker today after the therapy team met. They have recommended that Ashley stay a couple more weeks than the original plan. On one hand, this feels like a disappointment, especially since Ashley is telling us constantly she wants to go home. I can't say I blame her! I'd want to go home if I were her!

However, we really have to think about what will be best for Ashley's recovery. As much as it would be great to have her home, the level of therapy she gets at Madonna is very intense and may speed her recovery. And realistically, if she is home, she may be more comfortable, but we would have to transport her to/from therapy. Honestly, she is not very independent right now. Taking care of her is pretty demanding. So the therapists want to see her standing/walking/feeding herself and being a little more independent before she comes home. With an energetic 3-year-old waiting for Ashley at home, it might be a wise idea.

We will be talking with the therapists more the next couple days and weighing the decision about how to move forward. We'll pray for continued strength and that God guides us.

Love and Prayers,
Sondra, Tim, Ashley, Nicole

Day 41
11:49 p.m.

Footprints in the sand

Many of you are probably familiar with the famous poem "Footprints in the Sand." It's one of my favorites. The famous line at the end of the poem ...

During your times of trial and suffering when you saw only
one set of footprints it was then that I carried you ...

Today, there were moments when there were TWO sets of footprints in the sand! Yes, Ashley is trying very, very hard to get those legs working! And her dad has been working her really hard the last couple days!

When I came today, they had a special surprise. With Tim supporting Ashley under her arms, she was standing, putting weight on her feet and taking steps! It was very hard work for her and she even said that it hurt ... but at the same time she had huge smiles of pride and accomplishment. Tim was helping her a lot, but it was definitely Ashley doing the work to move those legs!

This child just never ceases to amaze us. We tell her to breathe without the help of a ventilator, and she does. We tell her to eat without a feeding tube, and she does. We tell her to speak so we can hear her beautiful voice, and she does. We tell her to walk so she can go home, and she does! She is just so determined!

I watched a documentary last night of Erik Weihenmayer, the blind climber who climbed Mount Everest (among 7 of the top summits he has climbed). Did you know that Erik and his team spent 1 1/2 months on Mount Everest before they finally made their first attempt to climb the final treacherous distance to the summit? It was a message to me that sometimes the most sought-after goals take time and patience, but if it's really worth it, it's worth the effort. Ashley is working on building the strength to "climb her summit."

We decided today that maintaining focus on the level of intense therapy Ashley is currently receiving is the best approach. So we'll take the therapists' advice and agree to continue her stay at Madonna. I expect that Ashley will excel in the upcoming weeks and the potential additional 2 week timeframe that may lie ahead could be less. We'll let Ashley determine the pace. Either way, we decided it will be better for all of us to see her progress a little farther before coming home! (She might be mad now, but someday she will understand!)

We'll keep you all posted on her progress. Can't wait until I get the chance to post pictures of Ashley standing on her own two feet, without our help.

Love and Prayers,
Sondra, Tim, Ashley, Nicole

Day 42
12:53 a.m.

Rock star day!

From wearing her "pair of dark sunglasses" for our walk outside, to her glittering "Pretty Lil Princess" t-shirt, to singing Beyonce songs in the hallway and watching "High School Musical" ... Ashley had a "rock star" day!

We had a great day today. She was quite interactive today. Lots going on in her head, and there are new things coming out in her speech every day. Sometimes they are random, confused thoughts. And I've even heard her whispering in her sleep. And it often takes her some time to "process" questions we ask her. It is apparent that her brain is healing and things are very busy in there trying to reconnect all her processing centers! And the great news is that we see so much of it coming back each day.

I found this excerpt from the book *My Stroke of Insight* to be an interesting description of what I believe Ashley must be experiencing:

"The effort it took for me to pay attention to what someone was saying was like the effort it takes to pay attention to someone who is speaking on a cell phone with a bad connection. You have to work so hard to hear what the person is saying that you may become impatient, frustrated, and hang up the phone. That's the kind of effort it took for me to hear a voice in a noisy background. It took a tremendous amount of willingness and determination on my part, and infinite patience on the part of the speaker."

Believe it or not, Ashley was singing and humming along to Beyonce's song today ("To the Left, To the Left" ... even singing the word "irreplaceable" which is a pretty big word). And she was singing it with heart and soul. Then she moved over to a favorite country tune and was singing "Love Your Baby Girl" by Sugarland, as we wheeled down the hallway! Both of these are familiar tunes to which Ashley and Nicole liked to sing along in Mom's car (and yes, I sang along with them—as bad as my voice might be—can't beat the surround sound in the car!).

The challenge is that a lot of Ashley's energy is being expended on these kinds of cognitive activities, which have now become "fun" for her. So I think she becomes easily frustrated with the "hard stuff" like walking! Nonetheless, she was working really hard today. I say "I can stand on my own..." and she says "two feet"! And she's workin' it!

Ashley got a little boost of encouragement when a couple of her favorite teachers from school visited today to cheer her on with a message of "we want you back at school, girlfriend!"

Ashley, you ARE A ROCK STAR!

Love and Prayers,
Sondra, Tim, Ashley, Nicole

Day 43
1:07 a.m.

Songwriter

We have a rock star in the family! And now we have a songwriter in the family too!! Nicole composed a song for Ashley, she informed us today. This is how it goes ...

I love my Ashee
I love my Ashee

And she sang it the same way numerous times today. So I think it is an actual tune!

Nicole and Mica came to visit and help Ashley in her therapy today. And Grandma Sharon came to start her 2-day shift. One of the therapists said she wished she didn't have to leave our room to go to her next appointment, because she was having so much fun! Ashley and Nicole were having a very giggly day!

It was a good day for Ashley overall. She's getting more comfortable in the school room sessions where she goes to interact with other kids. She's always the comedian calling everyone "dude." There are daily variations now: Cherry Nut Ball Dude ... Nut Ball Dude ... Chicken Nugget Dude ... Ice Cream Nut Ball Dude ... Pumpkin Patch Dude and many others. I guess it's the creative right brain for Ashley showing its strength! Nonetheless, it brings lots of smiles and laughs from everyone around her!

The flip side is that she struggles to gain focus and corral her random thought processes. And we are still unsure about her vision, which could still be inhibiting her. You never quite know when she's going to break into a round of ABC's, or counting by 5's, or Gee Whiz, or Twinkle Little Star. We think it's her way of gaining "control" of her environment by reverting to something familiar and comfortable instead of the things that are frustrating her. It's like watching her brain heal from the outside-in.

Ashley's finding her walking legs little by little. We've been doing the daily "brushing technique" that has really helped her get past the initial agitation and sensitivity to stimulus.

After about 3 weeks of doing this daily, she now lies calmly during the "brushing" and tells us it tickles. This treatment helps the brain reorganize its response to the external stimulus the body is receiving and reshape its boundaries. Next time I have a bad day, I'm going to get out Ashley's "brush" and give it a try!

Here's a cute little poem I like as a tribute to the wonderful bond Ashley and Nicole share as sisters:

> *sister will you ...*
> *make believe*
> *play dress-up*
> *let me be the princess*
> *tell me stories in the dark*
> *always be my friend*

Love and Prayers,
Sondra, Tim, Ashley, Nicole

Day 44
6:13 p.m.

Sea legs

Our little mermaid has found her "sea legs." Grandma Sharon has been with Ashley today. She had pool therapy and did the best she has done yet! Walking back and forth the length of the pool, jumping, and dancing in the water (to *High School Musical* tunes, which Ashley requested)!

We've talked to Ashley several times on the phone today. And it's just such a wonderful feeling, as Ashley sounds just like she's always sounded on the phone. I have a voicemail on my cell phone from Ashley and Nicole that I had saved from sometime a couple months ago when I was out of town for work. I happened to come across it a few weeks ago while we were waiting for Ashley to come out of one of the MRI tests to determine the status of her brain trauma. I remember having a major meltdown when I heard her voice on my phone.

Ever since that day, I have listened to that voicemail every day, longing to hear her sweet voice again. And for several weeks I couldn't stop myself from wondering if it would be possible again for her to speak to us ... even though I kept stopping myself and reminding myself to Believe and Expect the Miracle to happen. It is just music to my ears now to hear every word! It's like listening to a newborn baby coo. You just can't hear it enough! It is such a wonderful feeling.

I wish I could have been there today to see Ashley in the pool, but I can see the smiles in my mind! I stopped by the pediatric hospital to visit some other little ones that we've been praying for. Being in the hospital brought back a lot of memories from Ashley being there only a few weeks ago. Amazingly, it feels like it's been a really long time. And when I heard about Ashley's fun day in the pool today, I couldn't help thinking back to the hyperbaric oxygen/pressure treatments and her "dives" below sea level that, I have no doubt, helped prepare her brain for this amazing recovery process! It worked! Even though we didn't know it at the time ... and all we had to do was remain patient.

Love and Prayers,
Sondra, Tim, Ashley, Nicole

Day 45
12:33 p.m.

Tears of joy

Those who sow in tears will reap with songs of joy.
— Psalm 126:3

Grandma Sharon spent the morning with Ashley, and then Aunt Mary came over from Des Moines to spend a couple days with Ashley. When she saw Ashley standing and smiling her big smile at her, she burst into tears! Tears of Joy!! The last time Aunt Mary saw Ashley a couple weeks ago she was not talking and not even close to considering standing on her feet! So I thought it was significant that I found this scripture on the very same day.

Ashley was pretty exhausted from a very full week of therapy. So Saturday was a light day with only one therapy session scheduled. It will be good for her to have a break. She has been a very busy girl! It takes a lot of energy to re-establish all the brain circuitry to learn to talk, eat, walk, see, and hear ... all at the same time!

Love and Prayers,
Sondra, Tim, Ashley, Nicole

Day 46
11:46 p.m.

P-I-G

Ashley has always been a slender, wispy little girl. Well since she's been at Madonna, she has gained about seven pounds! (It's all the pudding and ice cream she's been eating!) So today we were remarking at how Ashley's getting a cute little pot belly (pot bellies are cute when you're only seven).

Aunt Mary says, "Well, Ashley's been eating like a little P-I-G" (spelling the word). And Ashley turned to her and said "Pig"! We all laughed so hard! Ashley's teachers will be happy to know that her spelling skills have come back!

Today was a calm day for Ashley with only two therapy sessions. She is getting much more comfortable on her feet, and not complaining anymore about walking. Although she still needs help from us to hold onto her arms and help give her support and balance. Aunt Mary's challenge to Ashley is to be walking five steps with no help before she visits next weekend. I think she can do it!

Today was a good day to be thankful and just live in the "present moment." Quote for today:

> If we fill our hours with regrets of yesterday and worries
> of tomorrow, we have no today in which to be thankful.

Love and Prayers,
Sondra, Tim, Ashley, Nicole

Day 47
10:23 p.m.

Snuggle bunny

Ashley had an awesome time hanging out with Aunt Mary the last few days! Mary, you are such a blessing to us and to Ashley! Not only did Ashley have a fun time singing, reading books, and laughing with you, but I know she worked hard for you too (like having to walk to get the ice cream!). We'll work on getting pool time next time you are here! When I arrived today, Ashley was playing word games with Aunt Mary and the Speech Therapist, and really doing well with answering questions.

Ashley was in a very snuggly mood, and when I asked her if she was a snuggle bug or a snuggle bunny, she picked bunny! She has always been a very affectionate child, very kind-hearted, loving, and caring. She has always been known for giving her teachers hugs and kisses! We also know that is one of her charming little strategies for wriggling out of having to do work!

A couple of the therapists were falling for Ashley's "snuggles" today, and Aunt Mary had to laugh and tell them what was really going on! So then Ashley had to get back to work!

You can imagine that when Mom arrived today, she was ready to give all the hugs and snuggles that she had stored up! And when I asked her what snuggle-bunnies ate (thinking she would say carrots), she whispered "chocolate pudding." She's a smart one!

Love and Prayers,
Sondra, Tim, Ashley, Nicole

Day 48
10:34 p.m.

Seashells

Instead of talking about going home today, Ashley kept saying, "I want to go to our orange house by the beach!" And when I would ask her, "Where is our orange house by the beach," she would say "Cabo."

When I asked her what we would do if we were there, she said, "Look for seashells!" There's a favorite place we have gone as a family in Cabo San Lucas, Mexico, and Ashley has always called it "our orange house by the beach" because it resembles an adobe structure. And looking for seashells is one of her favorite things to do!

I was very impressed with her memory and recollection of details of our family vacations. It truly warms my heart to know that she remembers special times such as this, and that the wonderful 7 years of her precious little life are not a loss as far as the special memories!

At one point she said that she wanted to take Grandma Sharon with us to the "orange house at the beach." When I asked her "who else?" she said, "our entire family!" I don't know exactly what she meant by that, but I have a feeling she wasn't talking about just Mom, Dad, Ashley, and Nicole!

Later in the day she said she wanted to "live at the orange house by the beach" and then added "forever!" Frankly, I wouldn't mind living at the "orange house by the beach forever," myself! I told her we'd have to discuss that one with Dad! Ironically, "going to the beach" was just the thing we all wished for at the waterfall in the pediatric hospital the morning of surgery! And I am confident we will go to the beach again, once Ashley has fully recovered and it will be a cherished vacation like none other.

Ashley had a really good day today, eating like a P-I-G again, walking (with about 25% assistance), swimming, singing songs, and playing Simon Says. She is also beginning to do some testing and therapy to help us understand what's going on with her vision. We believe that she can see, but we are not sure how well. It appears there is still more healing that needs to take place for her vision to function properly. She'll be seen by a specialist for her vision on Thursday.

We continue to BELIEVE that this will come together for her in time, in the same fashion that her other abilities have continued to come back to her. Please continue to pray for Ashley, and ask that God may heal her eyes so she can see the beauty and love around her.

Love and Prayers,
Sondra, Tim, Ashley, Nicole

Chapter Nine

I Can Walk on My Own Two Feet

Day 49
1:18 a.m.

Flashback

Ashley had a really great day today. It is really quite amazing, because yesterday was the original date that she was projected to be released. The motivation that she needed to be able to walk has really worked! Today she was walking down the hallways holding my hand (with my other hand on her back to help her balance). She is WALKING!

So now she has two more weeks to be WALKING BY HERSELF! So the new motto is, "I can walk on my own two feet ... all by myself!" Ashley recites it with pride! It's definitely hard work, as many of the Madonna staff witnessed today as Ashley was crying and yelling STOP! OWIE! as she was walking down the hallway with her physical therapist!

If she were an adult, she would have been cursing! It's that willpower and determination shining through! She is a fighter, I have no doubt! As she was napping after her therapies today, I was scanning through the text messages on my cell phone (only due to the "capacity is full" message), and I came across a number of text messages that had passed between friends and family during the most difficult moments of this journey.

Reading some of them brought flashbacks of the time we spent at the medical center for the hyperbaric treatments and the really "breakdown" emotional moments that we had. And it occurred to me that the reason we are able to experience such extreme joy at the smallest accomplishments day-by-day is that we've experienced the most "raw" emotions possible to experience. It's the transparency of wearing your emotions on the outside, and not hiding them. It's the feeling that there is something positive to be gained from this experience.

It occurred to me that many families we see at Madonna with injured loved ones are feeling much the same pain and range of emotions. It's life-changing. And so it really made me think about how it changes people. We are obviously not the first nor the last family to experience a trauma like this. I only hope that we can learn from this and grow as a family. And perhaps help others deal with their own tragedies.

There are no mistakes, no coincidences.
All events are blessings given to us to learn from.
— Elisabeth Kubler-Ross

When I pray, coincidences happen. When I stop praying, coincidences stop.
— William Temple, Archbishop of Canterbury

Love and Prayers,
Sondra, Tim, Ashley, Nicole

Day 50
12:08 a.m.

Brown-eyed girl

Ashley has the most beautiful brown eyes, and these long, thick eyelashes with little blond tips. Not only do I wish I had her long blond hair, but the eyelashes to go along with it! Now we are focused on getting those beautiful brown eyes seeing again!

When Ashley's brain injury occurred, I immediately thought about the loss of physical ability and cognitive ability. But the impact to vision was something that just never occurred to me. Ashley was seen today by an optometrist that works with Madonna. She did an observational assessment and determined that Ashley has partial vision right now. She is able to see objects placed to her lower left. But as the objects are placed in front of her and to her right, she begins to lose focus on them.

We have been told that the area of her brain that was injured is responsible for vision. Fortunately, she did not suffer any optic nerve damage. So, technically, her eyes are healthy, but her brain needs to continue to heal and the circuitry needs to be reconnected to regain her vision.

The doctor suggested several strategies for the therapists to work on with Ashley to re-train her eyes and brain. Looking at bright colors, going out into bright sunlight, wearing thick glasses for brief periods of time ... all of these things will help. I BELIEVE that this is Ashley's next area of focus, and like each other obstacle, we just need to focus our positive energy on her beautiful brown eyes, cheer her on with encouragement, and let that part of her brain heal.

As far as walking, she is mastering that beautifully! Tim and Ashley were walking everywhere today without the wheelchair (cafeteria and back, therapy gym and back, outside). And Ashley even did a couple dance moves while she was singing "Gee Whiz"! Wow! By the time Ashley comes home in two weeks, she'll be able to walk really well! Grandma Sharon is with Ashley tonight and was amazed today when she saw the improvement in her walking since just Sunday!

> *The greatest things in this world can't be seen*
> *or even touched—they must be felt with the heart.*
> *— Helen Keller*

> *The real voyage of discovery consists not in seeking*
> *new landscapes but in having new eyes.*
> *— Marcel Proust*

Love and Prayers,
Sondra, Tim, Ashley, Nicole

Day 51
8:20 p.m.

Dancin' shoes

Ashley spent the day with her Grandma Sharon. Ashley's been walking everywhere with Grandma Sharon. All the people at Madonna have been amazed at Ashley's sudden progress with her walking. I spoke with her educational specialist today, who usually sees Ashley in the Learning Center, and she's always been in her wheelchair. The educational specialist saw Ashley walking down the hallway today and was amazed!

She told me, "I had no idea she could walk like that! I've only seen her in a wheelchair."

Well, wheelchair no more! We are bringing down the dancing shoes, girlfriend!

The educational specialist told me she visited Ashley in her room later in the day, and she noticed Ashley's portrait on the wall of her from her dance recital. She mentioned to Ashley that she's fond of tap and ballet as well. She asked Ashley if she knows how to do a specific tap step. And Ashley replied, "Yes, and also a stepple-change."

Her teacher laughed, and said to dig out the tap shoes! Ashley also has been begun working on her "eye exercises," which she is protesting! We fondly call it willpower! She needs to wear her "goggles" (the funny looking thick glasses) for 5 minute intervals (with her eyes open, of course).

Grandma Sharon said that she noticed Ashley floating her hand around like a bird, while watching her hand. And holding up 1, 2, 3 fingers while watching them. It seems that she has a heightened sense of awareness about her ability to see after doing a few of the eye exercises. This is very encouraging.

I spoke with Ashley's school today and we scheduled a teleconference for Monday to gather her "team" from school and her "team" from Madonna to discuss the short-term plan for Ashley's educational needs. We anticipate that Ashley will participate in some home-based schooling while she continues her out-patient therapy and eventually work her way back to joining her 2nd grade class at school. We are so thrilled to be at this point of being able to even discuss Ashley's re-entry to school.

Every day brings more blessings! Thank you to everyone for the positive energy, prayers, and encouragement! And for being with us on this journey to witness a miracle in progress!

Love and Prayers,
Sondra, Tim, Ashley, Nicole

Day 52
11:31 p.m.

Family outing

One of Ashley's favorite foods is tacos and burritos! When she woke up this morning, she told Grandma Sharon she wanted a burrito to eat! So we had a family outing today that was Ashley's request. We went out to eat as a family at a Mexican restaurant! Our first family meal outside of a hospital for 52 days!

Today we officially started the countdown to Ashley's homecoming. Starting tomorrow, Ashley has ten more days before her discharge date! We are really, really looking forward to having our family under the same roof again very soon!

Men, fight for your sons, fight for your daughters,
fight for your wives, fight for your families.
If you will fight, then God will fight.
— Nehemiah 4:14

Love and Prayers,
Sondra, Tim, Ashley, Nicole

Day 53
10:31 p.m.

Countdown to homecoming

Ten more days at Madonna!

We are SO ready for Ashley to come home! This week, she will get to come home for half day on Wednesday for a home visit with her therapists. A couple of the therapists from Madonna will be coming to our home to help us identify any equipment, special needs, safety concerns for Ashley when she comes home. She will still need a lot of guidance and assistance once she's home from using the bathroom, to eating, to walking around. Particularly until her vision improves, it is kind of like guiding a blind person around.

We can see that there is improvement in her vision each day, so we BELIEVE that it will come back when that area of her brain heals and the circuits reconnect. All positive signs! And she repeats her new affirmation, "I can see with my own TWO EYES!!" (It worked with the standing and walking!)

Ashley had some fun visitors today from the neighborhood. She couldn't stop hugging and kissing everyone! Ashley is going to be so overjoyed to see her friends and neighbors when she gets home!

This week will be a busy week for us and for Ashley. She'll be working hard in her therapy. (Aunt Mary is sleeping over with Ashley tonight and tomorrow night, so that means Ashley's going to have to work extra hard! One of Ashley's therapists has tagged Mary with being responsible for encouraging Ashley to walk!) And Mary was certainly overjoyed to see that Ashley had exceeded her goal she set for her of five steps by herself!

Ashley has set a new goal for herself of 1,000 steps all by herself! She is DREAMING BIG! We will be working with her team at Madonna to prepare for her homecoming, plan for out-patient therapy, formulate a plan with school, and getting ready to simply celebrate!

If you BELIEVE, you will receive whatever you ask for in prayer.
— Matthew 21:22

Love and Prayers,
Sondra, Tim, Ashley, Nicole

We were disappointed when it was decided to extend Ashley's stay at Madonna by two more weeks. However, we also were hopeful that this additional time would give Ashley the extra time to master walking. There was a part of me that wanted her to come home. There was another part of me that was not prepared for her to come home in a wheelchair.

The focus on her rehabilitation had significantly shifted to helping her become more independent walking so that she could walk enough to come home without the wheelchair. At one point, we weren't so sure this was realistic. We forced ourselves to believe it could be possible.

Aunt Mary was committed to making it possible. We weren't there to witness it, but she told us how hard she pushed Ashley and how Ashley rose to the occasion and embraced the challenge. Chocolate pudding was the reward. She said Ashley pushed through the pain of walking for the sake of getting that chocolate pudding. It was an empowering experience for both of them.

Day 54
11:22 p.m.

Teamwork!

Nine more days at Madonna!

Teamwork has been the theme since the beginning of Ashley's journey! We entered this endeavor as a family, a team fully prepared for victory! The team that performed Ashley's surgery ... the teams of people there to support Ashley at The Nebraska Medical Center and pediatric ICU, the team continuing to care for her in therapy, nurses, and the incredible team of doctors, nurses and therapists and Madonna, and now we are anticipating an out-patient therapy team and a team of people working with Ashley at school. And not to mention the incredible cheering section she has had!

We continue to be overwhelmed by the number of lives our young child has touched and how wonderful and caring people are about helping her get better so she can fulfill her life dreams!

Today, in the spirit of true teamwork, a teleconference was held between the school and Madonna rehab teams ... 15 people in all! With one single focus of discussion: Ashley, our miracle girl! It was very interesting to witness the discussion from a more "observational" and "clinical" descriptive perspective. Hearing the therapists explain to the educational team where Ashley's brain injury occurred and how specifically that has impaired her vision, and other functions.

The great news is that everyone continues to have an extremely optimistic attitude about Ashley's ability to gain everything back in time. And the level of intensity in treatment everyone agrees is something in which we need to continue to stay focused. So, as we continue to evaluate the out-patient therapy options, we will be looking for a very intense approach.

The best part will be having Ashley home with us. We'll fly her to the moon and back for therapy if we need to, so long as we can have her home with us! Can you only imagine the feeling you have of sleeping in your own bed after you've been away on an extended business trip or vacation? Doesn't it just always feel better to sleep in your own bed? Ashley's time is coming! She might just sleep for days once she's in her own bed!

Aunt Mary is graciously staying with Ashley again tonight. She and Ashley have been working hard today going through the daily routine of multiple therapies. Again, we are blessed to have the help and support of our families.

Love and Prayers,

Sondra, Tim, Ashley, Nicole

Day 55
10:53 p.m.

School daze

8 more days at Madonna!

Tonight is the eve of the first day back to school for Ashley's school. While many of the kids in the neighborhood are tucked into bed early, backpacks were ready, and new clothes layed out for the first day, we await Ashley's return home. It's hard to even think about school starting, as it feels like our summer has not even started! I am reminded of fond memories of Ashley's first day of kindergarten and 1st grade. And I've refrained from buying a single pencil for school supplies, as I'm determined that together, with Ashley, we'll pick out her backpack and school supplies!

Even though Ashley won't start school tomorrow, it is still a milestone day, as she will be coming home for the day for a preparatory visit with her therapist. The therapist will spend a couple hours here to help us identify any special needs or safety concerns for Ashley when she comes home. It will be so exciting to have her home for the day! I just hope that it won't be difficult for her to go back to Madonna, even though it will only be for a few more days. She's been working hard, and her spirits have been good.

> *In dreams and love there are no impossibilities.*
> — *Janos Arany*

Love and Prayers,
Sondra, Tim, Ashley, Nicole

Day 56
10:09 p.m.

Looking homeward

7 more days at Madonna!

Ashley spent today "practicing" for her homecoming, and the next "chapter" in her recovery. Tim drove her home this morning. We spent a couple hours with the therapist going on a tour and discussing potential obstacles that Ashley might encounter, such as lighting, steps, picking up rugs, etc. And then we had the rest of the day to "chill-out" before we drove Ashley back to Lincoln.

Ashley was pretty mellow today and seemed to enjoy relaxing in the comfort and quiet of home (other than wanting to watch "Dora" and "Handy

Manny" cartoons over and over!). Benny her dog has obviously missed her, as he wanted to be right by her side all day!

The visit today was somewhat overwhelming, from my perspective, as it brought to light the level of assistance Ashley is going to need when she comes home, and the reality of juggling her needs along with a very energetic, independent 3-year-old! As much as we are overjoyed about having Ashley come home, it's also apparent that she still has a lot of healing and therapy to do.

It's sad to admit that we can't just snap our fingers, have her home, and have everything be as it was before. It's just going to continue to take time, and we'll continue to adapt with each new step.

After considering several out-patient options, we decided today that we will continue to take Ashley to Madonna in Lincoln to participate in their All-Day Out-patient Rehab program. Although this seems like an "inconvenience" to drive back and forth to Lincoln every day, in the long run, we decided the intense level of therapy she is receiving at Madonna is so important right now.

The upside is that Ashley will be home to sleep in her bed every night and home on the weekends. And she won't have any more doctors or nurses doing "vital signs" every few hours (not that we don't appreciate their care). The focus for the day program will purely be on therapy. So we'll have to just take this a week at a time. Ashley's progress will be the indicator for when we can make a transition to a less intense out-patient program. We have some good options, once she's ready for that.

Ashley was visited today by many of our friends in the neighborhood and was very happy to see everyone! The best of all is a picture of her "standing on her own two feet" in front of our house!

She was in good spirits tonight when we got back to Madonna. Nicole had a rather challenging day today (late to bed, early to rise, and not a long enough nap!). When Grandma Sharon asked Nicole if she had a rough day, Ashley commented gleefully, yeah she did, but not me! Ashley's focused on coming home!! She handled it well that she had to go back to stay for a few more days ... and she won't let us forget that she's coming home next Wednesday!

Love and Prayers,
Sondra, Tim, Ashley, Nicole

*Ashley was so proud to stand in our driveway
and greet her neighborhood friends.*

Coping Strategies: Slow Down and Focus on One Thing at a Time

When faced with a tragic situation such as what we experienced, we discovered that life simply must slow down. There will be missed activities and commitments and appointments. People will understand. This is a time to conserve your energy. Multi-tasking and trying to juggle the typical daily demands will only consume energy your brain needs to process a stressful situation.

As I stated earlier, focus your energy one minute, hour, or day at a time. During Ashley's rehabilitation, what we focused on ended up being where she focused. We used mantras and I highly recommend them. Some of them were, "I can stand on my own two feet." "I can walk on my own two feet." "I can see with my own two eyes." "Two arms are better than one." We would recite them over and over. And eventually she began reciting them with us.

We tried not to look too far beyond the next stage of healing. We kept thinking about the next milestone. This helped the scope of the rehabilitation process and the magnitude of her having to re-learn everything seem less daunting.

For we live by faith, not by sight.

— 2 Corinthians 5:7

Look at everything as though you were seeing it either for the first or last time. Then, your time on earth will be filled with glory.

— Betty Smith

Chapter Ten

I Can See with My Own Two Eyes

Day 57
11:59 p.m.

Better than the day before

6 more days at Madonna!

"In six days LORD made everything … On the seventh day he rested."
— Exodus 20:11

I think that must be what Ashley is looking forward to doing, because she is very much aware of how many days she has left before coming home. She is very focused on the "countdown." And it IS amazing what can happen in six days or less. Ashley said today that she can see better than she could see yesterday.

The therapist that was working with Ashley on her vision today also confirmed that Ashley's vision was improving. She was holding objects up and Ashley was reaching accurately for them … in all directions. This is so wonderful, because improvement in Ashley's vision will help her with so many other areas of recovery and in her transition home.

Tim has been saying, "Ashley's vision will be a whole lot better before she comes home. She's got seven whole days." I must admit that I "caught myself" thinking that was wishful thinking. And then I realized that Tim's BELIEF was not wavering … and neither should mine. Ashley has done amazing things through this recovery process, in less than a week's time! She is a hard worker! And very determined!

Love and Prayers,
Sondra, Tim, Ashley, Nicole

These fashionable red-framed glasses with thick lenses were designed to "exercise" Ashley's eyes to help her vision return.

Day 58
10:15 p.m.

Aha moment!!

5 more days at Madonna!

Tonight I was sitting here rocking with Ashley (one of her favorite things to do at the end of a hard day's work!). We were chatting and singing. We called Tim, because Ashley wanted to talk to her "napp'n partner!" He's on a weekend fishing trip and Ashley wanted to know if he was going to "eat" the fish IF he caught them! He said no, that he would throw them back and let them swim away. She laughed as though she thought that was rather silly! So glad that Tim went on the trip. He deserves a break.

And so a little later on, I picked up a magazine and said, "Hey, Ashley, can you see this picture?" "Nope," she said.

Again, I said, "Can you see this magazine I'm holding in front of you?" "Nope," she said.

So I said, "Ashley, who is this picture of?" "OPRAH," she says!

I just about flipped out of the chair!! Yes, indeed, it was an *Oprah* magazine with a life-sized picture of Oprah on the front cover. Now, if any of you know that I am, myself, an Oprah fan, you'll remember that I'm always using her lingo and talking about "Aha moments." Well this most certainly was an "Aha moment." Because it was never more clear that Ashley could not only see, but she could interpret what she saw, and she could even name the person who, extraordinarily, she has never even met!

I'm going to declare, right now, that there will be a day in this child's life that she will sit on the stage next to Oprah! And I only hope that when she does, she'll be gracious enough to let her mom join her! If Oprah only knew the impact she has had on a 7-year-old girl recovering from brain trauma and her mother ... that's what you call someone who is not only famous, but is leaving her mark on the world. And Ashley is doing that already too! This moment has topped my list of Aha moments!

You're sons of Light, daughters of Day. We live under wide open
skies and know where we stand. So let's not sleepwalk through life.
— 1 Thessalonians 5:5-6

The one predominant duty is to find one's work and to do it.
— Charlotte Perkins Gilman

Life is a gift from God, and we must treasure it, protect it, and invest it.
— Warren Wiershe

Ashley, dear girl, you inspire me to be my very best! And you always do it while making me laugh!

Love and Prayers,
Sondra, Tim, Ashley, Nicole

I knew Ashley's vision was returning when she remarkably identified that Oprah was pictured on the cover of the magazine I was holding in front of her.

Day 59
11:35 p.m.

Stupendous

4 more days at Madonna!

"Stupendous" was the word of the day today! Don't know where it came from, but Ashley kept saying it! And it was a stupendous day, indeed. Ashley had three therapy sessions this morning, and she actually "requested" that she work on going up and down the stairs! (She knows she's got a flight of seventeen stairs to conquer to sleep in her own bed once she gets home!) Then we played Hide-N-Seek, and she found me hiding in the therapy gym ... by only using her eyes! Not my voice!

Ashley and I went on an outing this afternoon. We visited our friends and went on a picnic with them. Ashley walked quite a long distance to the picnic shelter. She was a little tired, and maybe a little overwhelmed by the "big blue sky" in contrast to her cozy little room at Madonna.

After lunch she tackled the playground with help from her friends! Ashley "climbed the ladder" and went down the slide three times! Don't worry. We helped and coached her every step of the way. I think I had more fear letting her go down the slide than she did!! (The pride I felt watching Ashley climb and go down the slide today may have matched the pride Michael Phelps's mother felt watching him win his eighth gold medal tonight!)

Afterward, we went for a drive, Ashley listened to music and dozed a little and then we got chocolate milkshakes! She wasn't thrilled about going back to Madonna, as she kept saying, "Let's walk to your car and go for a ride again." It really did feel good to have the "freedom" to be away from the hospital, and to be able to spend the day spontaneously! We had a "stupendous" day, indeed!

All things are possible for the one who believes.
— Mark 9:23

A possibility is a hint from God.
— Soren Kierkegaard

Love and Prayers,
Sondra, Tim, Ashley, Nicole

Day 60
11:52 p.m.

Shake your booty

3 more days until HOME!

It's been 60 days! A little more than two calendar months. One sixth of a year. A blink of an eye in the span of Ashley's life ahead! Yet we continue to feel amazed at the magnitude of what we have experienced as a family during this time.

I realize that we are not unique, in that many people experience traumas in their lives. We know not the source or depth of our strength until we are forced to draw on it. Kind of like putting money in a savings account. You hope that there will be enough there should you ever need to draw on it. Except that in times like these, you have no choice but to make your resources stretch as long as needed. It's the kindness of friends and even strangers that makes the deposits into your moral support bank that keeps you going! And more importantly the endless depth of love!

Today, Ashley was in good spirits. She was frequently talking about going home! Ashley's grandparents and aunt visited today. Ashley and Nicole put on a dancing program. Ashley played her Hannah Montana guitar and had a pretty good rhyme going, while Nicole danced. They laughed and giggled and kept saying "shake your booty." They laughed even harder when they saw me shakin' my booty!

It is so great to see Ashley being a "kid" again! I think she will really excel once she's home. And it's great to just laugh and be silly as a family!

Tim enjoyed his fishing/camping trip this weekend and said he "bust a gut" laughing. His work buddies are a bunch of practical jokers; Tim fits right in. It's good for the soul to laugh! Glad he went and had a good time!

Take time to laugh. It is the music of the soul.
— Anonymous

Love and Prayers,
Sondra, Tim, Ashley, Nicole

Standing and walking in therapy is hard work. But standing just because she wants to play was a fun, new experience for Ashley.

Day 61

12:12 a.m.

Believing in miracles

2 more days at Madonna!

How many of you have witnessed a miracle? I, for one, can say I have. And now you can too.

We began this journey with a specific mission and have taken an unexpected detour. In the greatest moments of despair we began to speak the words ... BELIEVE. BELIEVE. BELIEVE. We told ourselves to "Expect a Miracle." We wore bracelets, necklaces, and even tattooed our bodies to remind ourselves of the power of faith, hope, love, and unwavering belief.

From the days we talked about the angels in the room, we knew there was something special happening. I still recall that morning driving to the hospital for Ashley's surgery, the feeling that we were "floating." It was as if we were riding on angels' wings.

Someone asked me today how Ashley's heart was doing? And we talked about how it's almost hard to remember that was the reason we began this journey! We can honestly say that we never, in a million years, would have expected this would be the path we would end up taking.

However, there has been a lot of good that has come from this journey ... realization of priorities, family bonds, unconditional love, value of friendship, and the simple things in life. I wish I could place those good feelings in a bottle and open it now and then to remind us where we've been or to share with a friend in despair. There's a lot that we'd just as well forget about this journey. But there's also a lot that I hope we never forget!

Two more nights ... and we will ALL be sleeping in our own beds! For 61 days, we've kept our nightly vigil of always having someone stay with Ashley. She's never been alone on this journey. Our Belief from the beginning (even when she was comatose) was that Ashley would heal if she felt our love and support surrounding her. The pictures now speak for themselves! She is the bright, shiny, happy star at the end of this journey!! A true Miracle of God.

Love is the divine reality that everywhere produces
and restores life. To each and every one of us,
it gives the power of working miracles if we will.
— Lydia Maria Child

With God's Power working in us,
God can do much, much more than
anything we can ask or imagine.
— Ephesians 3:20

Love and Prayers
Sondra, Tim, Ashley, Nicole

P.S.: I forgot to mention there is now a 6th member of the "BELIEVE TATTOO TEAM." My Dad, Larry, got his tattoo a couple weeks ago!

Day 62
12:07 a.m.

Super girl!

"Tomorrow I am going home!"

Ashley said those words to EVERYONE she saw at Madonna today!! She got to bake brownies with her occupational therapist (it was hard for her to understand that they needed to bake first before eating them). Ashley handed out brownies to all her nurses and therapists to say thank you!

In her morning therapy session, she was flexing her muscles and saying, "I'm SUPER GIRL. I'm strong!" And by the end of the day, she was saying, "I'm SUPER GIRL, I'm strong! I can do anything!"

I BELIEVE, Ashley that you CAN do anything you set your mind to do! As you can see she got a lot of encouragement and accolades from her fans at Madonna today! Even the cooks in the cafeteria were cheering for Ashley today!

Of course, the true princess she is ... she was kissing and hugging everyone. And telling me, "I like being nice to people." Ashley has always been an affectionate, happy child and she has a very gracious heart. Her personality has persevered through this traumatic experience. My self-esteem is always greatly improved after spending a day around Ashley.

So many times in the early weeks of our journey, I longed to hear her tell me, "Mom you're pretty, I love you." Now I get to hear those words repeatedly, along with, "You smell good," "You are my best friend," "You make the best soup." This is one area where the perseverative behavior (that still exists as part of her brain's healing process) is just fine with me!

Tomorrow morning we'll have breakfast, say our goodbyes, and go HOME!

Character cannot be developed in ease and quiet. Only through
trial and suffering is the soul strengthened.
— Helen Keller

We also have joy with our troubles, because we know that these
troubles produce patience. And patience produces character,
and character produces hope.
— Romans 5:3-4

Love and Prayers,
Sondra, Tim, Ashley, Nicole

Life Lesson: Appreciate the Now

I remember very vividly the pain of missing the moments I had with my daughter, during those darkest hours in which I didn't know if we would have a chance to create more like them. It was painful to think about the times that I was "too busy" to read a book or play outside. And when all of my "predictions" of what the future would look like were removed, I had nothing to hang onto. All I had was now. All I had was to cherish the moment—to be grateful for each additional breath and each small step to recovery for my daughter and my family.

" Dare to believe—because believing makes it so! "

— Beth Mende Conny

" The mind determines what's possible. The heart surpasses it. "

— Pilar Coolinta

Chapter Eleven

Home Sweet Home

Day 63
11:31 p.m.

Home sweet home!!

We are HOME! Joy! Peace! Elation!

I can't begin to tell you how wonderful this day has been! Ashley woke up at 6:30 am and the first words she spoke were, "I want to go home!" I replied, "Okay"!

"I want to go home RIGHT NOW," she said. I said "Okay!"

It was such a great feeling to finally be able to say, "Yes, we can go home now!" So we got ready, finished packing up, ate breakfast, signed the discharge paperwork, said our happy goodbyes and we were HOME by 10 am this morning! And Ashley has been smiling ever since!

We spent a good portion of the day unpacking, settling in, and rearranging some things so that it would make it easier for Ashley to move around the house. Her vision has improved even since her home visit last week, but she still moves slowly and is somewhat timid. She needs some guidance and assistance. She can see objects in front of her, but may not be focusing or interpreting everything properly yet. We are confident the improvements will continue.

It was a beautiful, sunny, mild day today. So we spent some time this evening outdoors with neighborhood friends. Ashley was at the center of all the kids, just having a blast. They were all so happy to see her home and so very kind and caring. They helped her play hide and seek, and duck, duck, goose, and all I could hear were giggles and laughter! Music to my ears!!

I really BELIEVE that Ashley's continued recovery will really accelerate now that she is home and able to spend time with familiar friends and with other kids! She was sitting down, standing up, doing a lot of things that have been challenging for her to do. But I think when she's playing and having fun, she forgets about it being hard, and she does things without even thinking about it! And when she's ready to go back to school, I think she'll continue to make rapid progress.

The journey is certainly not over ... but it's beginning to feel like it won't last forever.

I'm going to share a secret with you all. Some may think it's weird. Those that are highly sentimental or mothers will relate. I have had the pair of pajamas Ashley wore to the hospital in my overnight bag since the day she wore them to the hospital for surgery. They haven't been washed, and each time I picked them up to throw them in the laundry, I put them right back in my bag. For some reason, I just couldn't bring myself to wash them until she was home.

Tonight, they are in the laundry basket! And we are all sleeping under the same roof, as a family, for the first time in 63 days! Ashley and Nicole are asleep in their OWN beds, dreaming sweet dreams!

A joyful heart is like a sunshine of God's love, the hope of eternal happiness, a burning flame of God ... And if we pray, we will become that sunshine of God's love—in our own home, the place where we live, and in the world at large.
— *Mother Teresa*

Love and Prayers,
Sondra, Tim, Ashley, Nicole

Having our family back together at home had become such a priority for us during our sixty-three-day journey. It literally felt like paradise to all be sleeping under the same roof again. It was such a joy to tuck Ashley and Nicole into bed together and watch them snuggle and hear their giggles. Once they were asleep, I took pictures of them. It was as if I needed "evidence" that they were really together at home, sleeping in the same bed! They looked like sleeping angels.

Little sleepy angels at home in bed.

First Day After Discharge from Madonna Rehabilitation Hospital

A new chapter

Today we started a new chapter. The first chapter was the surgery and time at two hospitals. Chapter two was Ashley's rehab at Madonna. And now our new chapter is about Ashley's continued out-patient recovery at home.

I know there will be many more chapters in her recovery process. And we'll continue to take each one in stride. I know we will always be able to look back on this time and think of the lessons we have learned. I also think there will be a time that we can look back on this time and think, WOW, we made it through.

So now, we'll begin to focus on the future! A lot of people have asked that we continue to keep them informed about Ashley's progress and continued recovery. I have decided to keep the online journal going. There's no more "countdown to come home." So I may not update everyday ... we have lots to focus on now! (Plus I need to work on Ashley's letter to Oprah!)

I enjoy using this tool as a way to journal Ashley's story. There may be a day in the future that Ashley will want to read this and understand how she got to be such an amazing young girl. I also feel blessed that we have been able to share our story and bring inspiration to so many people.

Ashley has more than 400 guests registered on this online journal. And there had been over 10,000 visits to the online journal. That is absolutely amazing to me! I know all the prayers that have come about because of this tool have played a significant role in bringing about the positive energy to help her heal! I truly BELIEVE that! Little did I know that reading the book *The Secret* would be one of the most meaningful books I have ever read and actually applied to LIFE!

Life is not always what one wants it to be, but to make the best of it,
as it is, is the only way of being happy.
— Jennie Jerome Churchill

Love and Prayers,
Sondra, Tim, Ashley, Nicole

Life Lesson: There Is Nothing More Important Than Spending Time with the People You Love

As I reflected on this experience, I realized that one theme continued to override all others. It was the importance of family in my life. It's easy to take people for granted until you are faced with the potential of losing them. In our case, we knew that surgery for our daughter would be inevitable. So having the surgery wasn't a shock. However, we had convinced ourselves that this procedure that was expected to be "routine" would come and go and we'd continue living our lives.

When things didn't go according to that plan, every other struggle and frustration about life melted away. For sixty-three days we prayed for nothing more that the healing of our daughter and the reassembly of our family. I believe in that period of sixty-three days, our family also healed.

part three

Getting Back to Living

"
LIFE IS TOO SHORT to wake up in the morning with regrets. So love the people who treat you right, forgive the ones who don't and believe that everything happens for a reason. If you get a chance, take it. If it changes your life, let it.
— Harvey MacKay
"

" **To accomplish great things, we must not only act, but also dream, not only plan, but also BELIEVE.** "

— Anatole France

Chapter Twelve

Day Rehab

*J*ust as we had anticipated, Ashley began to THRIVE at home!
We felt like parents of a newborn child in awe of every new
thing she showed us.

"Look she's jumping and her feet actually left the floor! Look,
she's running!"

As Ashley's vision continued to come back day by day, so did
her sense of security and independence. She enjoyed just walking
around the house from room to room. She would say she was
"exercising her legs."

One evening, Nicole was "chasing" her around the kitchen,
and Ashley was actually running. It was a kind of awkward,
crooked little run, but she was running and laughing the whole
way. How wonderful to hear the giggles of both of our girls filling
the house. It was music to our ears!

We cherished the time being together at home as a family. We
were finally able to have a birthday party for Nicole. And resume
doing some of our favorite family activities like our Friday night
sand volleyball league.

Within those first few days, we were able to attend church as a
family for the first time in several months. It was such a blessing.
When we arrived, we were ushered to the very front row of
church. I was thinking to myself, *oh boy, this might be a disaster.*

Nicole was a little angel, and Ashley pranced proudly to the front of church and danced before God and the entire congregation during the music at the end of the service. It was wonderful to be together as a family and to witness my precious girl dance as if no one was watching.

I came across a poem about why God made little girls and thought that it matched perfectly with what we felt those first few days home ... PARADISE! Here are a few lines:

He was pleased and proud of the job He'd done
For the world, when seen through a little girl's eyes
Greatly resembles PARADISE.

— Arthur E. Knight

We were home, but Ashley's healing journey was still continuing. She no longer needed to be under constant in-patient medical care, but there was still a lot of therapy to do to regain all the strength and abilities that had been lost. Life still wouldn't return to normal just yet, and at that point in time I don't think we were really sure what "normal" meant anymore.

We began the daily trek back and forth to Madonna for Ashley to participate in the Day Rehab program. We took turns each day, Monday through Friday, taking her to Lincoln for an intense therapy schedule that lasted from nine to four each day. Tim had gone back to working as an electrician. Although I attempted to plug back into my work as a technology sales consultant, my mind just wasn't in it. We would continue to do what we needed to do and trust that the healing would continue for Ashley.

Amazingly, Ashley was full of energy wanting to play, run, explore, and laugh! It was great to see her stamina coming back. I couldn't help thinking back and looking at some of the pictures where she could barely keep her eyes open during therapy. I was just so impressed with how much she was becoming herself again!

Appreciate the now

At one point, Ashley started asking a lot more questions. "Is my birthday over?" "Mom, when is your birthday?" "Are we going to see fireworks again?" "How long was I in the hospital?"

I can only imagine that as her brain continued to heal and wake up, her awareness of the events that unknowingly passed her by, and the "summer that was lost," were beginning to come back to her. I doubt that she remembers very much, but she certainly knows she is not at the hospital anymore ... and she's living life LARGE!

With several birthdays and a holiday passing us by without much fanfare, we decided to make an extra special event out of the Labor Day Weekend. So we visited with family in Columbus and spent the night at a family member's cabin by a lake.

Ashley and Nicole played at the "beach," went swimming, caught fish, pretended to catch more fish, napped in a hammock, rode a boat, roasted marshmallows over a campfire, and slept in sleeping bags. (Now in case any of you are marveling at the notion of me camping, remember this was "indoor" camping—in a cabin! Nonetheless, to Ashley and Nicole, it was a "camping trip"!)

We had a great time, just relaxing and being together as a family! Ashley was doing just AMAZING! She is becoming more independent ... even reeling in the fishing pole with her weaker right hand.

Ashley kept asking to go home because there was a certain toy that she said she wanted to play with ... a toy instrument. I found myself saying, "Ashley, you can play with that toy anytime. How many days do you get to spend at a cabin by a lake?"

Ashley even brought up the fact that "we have to go back to Madonna tomorrow for therapy." And Nicole wanted to sit in the cabin and watch "Nemo." Again, I said, "You can watch cartoons any day. How many days do you get to be at a cabin?"

Then it occurred to me ... I was encouraging them to live in the moment; appreciate the "now"!! I thought about how many times I've read that and told myself I would do better practicing "being in the present" ... especially when I am with my kids! I even stopped wearing a watch for that very reason (or maybe it was that I really didn't need to know what time it was when I was on hospital duty twenty-four by seven).

So for a moment, I felt proud that I was not only practicing this skill I had been trying to improve, I was teaching it to my children! After all, that's what kids are supposed to do—just be kids and live in the moment, with no worries or cares.

Some Quotes to Enjoy:

When you run so fast to get somewhere, you miss half the fun of getting there. When you worry and hurry through your day, it is like an unopened gift ... thrown away. You better slow down, don't dance so fast, time is short, the music won't last.
— Author Unknown

We are often so caught up in our destination that we forget to appreciate the journey, especially the goodness of the people we meet along the way. Appreciation is a wonderful feeling, don't overlook it.
— Author Unknown

Love and Prayers,
Sondra, Tim, Ashley, Nicole

Do you remember the mantra we started during Ashley's inpatient rehabilitation, "I can see with my own two eyes"? On one particular day, I experienced a moment that revealed to me yet another request for Ashley's healing had been granted! She and I were eating lunch at Madonna one day during her Day Rehab, enjoying a beautiful day outdoors.

She said nonchalantly to me, "Mom, look at that butterfly." At first, I said, "Uh-huh." And then I realized the magnitude of what she had just said! I looked up and, sure enough, there was a tiny little white butterfly fluttering around the flowers. It reminded me of a day a few weeks prior when I had watched Nicole chasing a similar white butterfly. I truly believed these were signs from God reminding us to cherish the precious moments we have with our loved ones. These moments I once thought were mere coincidences, really were not coincidences at all!

Later, that same afternoon, we were walking outside during a break from therapy and again Ashley pointed to a bunch of pink flowers. This time it was a bumble bee that had caught her eye. That evening it was a tiny black cricket hopping across the sidewalk. Ashley has always loved little critters of all kinds: bugs, worms, spiders. Nothing has really ever frightened her except that she has an aversion to fallen, dead leaves. I find this to be oddly ironic.

Ashley's progress was absolutely remarkable. A friend asked me how much I thought Ashley had regained. My answer, at that time, was easily 80 percent. We had seen incredible improvement with her vision; she was now seeing colors. And attaching the correct labels to them! Before leaving Madonna, Ashley was seen by the vision specialist, whose reaction literally was, "WOW, WOW, WOW." Up until that point in time it hadn't appeared that Ashley could recognize colors.

Tim and I discussed our concern with the doctor, and she explained that the eyes are probably "seeing" colors, but the signals from the eyes to the brain might be confused and the right labels are not being associated with the color. We discussed some strategies to work on this. Four days later, Ashley was consistently naming colors, shapes, letters, and numbers. And she was beginning to read again. We had sent the signal out, and the universe had responded.

One night the girls stood outside in their PJ's on a crisp, cool fall evening and looked at the big, bright, full moon. Ashley looked up and saw the stars and suggested we all make wishes. A few weeks prior, she probably wouldn't have been able to see the moon. At that moment, she could see the tiniest twinkling stars!

This time she wished we could go back to "the cabin." This made me think of the day we threw coins in the water at the pediatric hospital, and she wished we could go to the beach. I think the main theme is that we are creating fondly treasured memories with our children that will last a lifetime. Someday when they are forty and wish upon a star, it will probably be for something very different. I only hope every once in a while they'll make a wish and remember the specialness of family bonds that this experience created for all of us.

With a lot of courage and belief in herself, Ashley was able to do all the things she was able to do that we had prayed so hard over the past sixty-three days she would do again. It really, truly was interesting to watch the speed at which the brain was healing itself.

It was not long before Ashley was going up and down the slide, riding her bike, and swinging.

While the first sixty-three days seemed to be an eternity, it was evident that there had been almost a methodical process of healing. It was like one center of the brain healed itself (based perhaps on where we were funneling the energy), and then the next, and so on. I was in awe of the fact that Ashley had re-learned virtually everything in the span of sixty-three days that had taken her six years to develop. It really was very intriguing. Imagine what we could train our brains to do if we only provided the focused energy to set goals and achieve them!

Ashley's overall strength and balance had improved as well. She even broke out her tap shoes in physical therapy! They were like "magic slippers." We put them on her, turned on the "Gee Whiz, I'm in Showbiz" music, and she began dancing her dance recital routine! She was moving her weaker right leg to all the moves without hesitation. Her therapist and I were in awe, my mouth dropped to the floor! I couldn't believe that Ashley could remember each and every dance step.

What was next? Got to get that right arm working. We knew that it worked and that Ashley could use her right hand, but she would say, "It's too hard." She preferred to use her left hand. This had become very functional for her and she could get by. The only problem was that Ashley was right-handed. We either needed to help her become left-dominant or focus on the healing of the right-hand movement. This would have the most impact on her ability to write and thus affect her participation in school. Our mantra for this stage of healing became, "Two arms are better than one."

As with all the other healing that we had seen from the "outside-in" with Ashley's brain, I believed she would regain complete use of her right, dominant hand. The therapists had noted that she had intuitive understanding of how to write letters and the proper spacial placement; however, the control wasn't there yet. Once the "pathways" reconnected, like the other "compartments" of her healing brain, I believed we would see sudden and rapid progress in this area as well. It was something that she continued to work on.

We continued our trek to Lincoln each day for therapy. They were long days. Sometimes Nicole came along to provide "encouragement." We began to discuss Ashley's re-entry plan for school and whether we would continue therapy in Lincoln or move to a program in Omaha.

We met with the Madonna therapy team and the elementary school teams, about fifteen people in all. We agreed on a plan for Ashley to complete her daily therapy at Madonna and "graduate" from their program. Then, Ashley would begin school. She would be joining her school mates about two months later than they had started school.

It was discussed that she would initially go for the morning, while continuing medical-based therapy in the afternoons in Omaha. We would continue to make adjustments based on her progress. In the meantime, we had school shopping to do. Ashley reminded me that we needed to buy notebooks and crayons and that her backpack had a hole in it. It was wonderful to think of Ashley going back to school. I recalled my breakdown day in the back-to-school aisle at the department store. I felt grateful now, and I realized that it was God's plan all along.

Ashley began to share the gifts of her gracious heart. One day, she sat down to play with a crying baby boy at Madonna who was recovering from his own brain injury. She sat right down and said, "Come here, it's okay." He stopped crying, looked at her, and smiled. She was so proud that she had cheered him up! And the little boy's mom and therapist both thanked her.

We then had to stop to visit an angel dog in the hallway! Ashley showered her with hugs and then asked if we could bring Benny to Madonna to visit people.

When we learned of a little boy in the hospital with a tragic head injury he received playing football, Ashley didn't hesitate for a second when I asked if she would be okay with going to visit his family. I told her that it was important for this little boy's family to see her, and that she is a miracle of healing.

Despite the two months she spent in the hospital, she didn't even flinch when we entered the hospital and the ICU to find the boy's family. Both of our girls are such angels from God! How many of us spend our lives wondering "what is my purpose?" I have no doubts that these two angels have an amazing purpose in this world!

90 days post-surgery

Hope

Ashley had her first follow-up appointment with the neurologist (after a full day of rehab and pool therapy at Madonna). It was the first time she walked in the doors of the pediatric hospital since she had left a couple months ago. Notice I said "walked!"

The first thing Ashley wanted to do was make wishes in the water stream! So she wished to go "back to the beach" and to go "back to the cabin" and to go "back to Florida," and to go back to the "orange house by the beach." Does this girl like to travel or what! I remember the days when all she wanted was to just "Go HOME!"

We visited a few special friends at the hospital. We stopped by to say hi to her surgeon, but he was busy fixing another little child's heart. Everyone we saw was amazed at the Ashley that was standing before them, compared to the Ashley they last saw!

The neurologist had only seen Ashley when she was at the pediatric hospital and The Nebraska Medical Center, so he spent a fair amount of time with us recalling the events and dates of her injury and recovery. As we answered the questions and filled in the neurologist, it was also a reflective moment. It was pretty amazing to think about how far she had come.

Meanwhile, Ashley played "Doctor" with the medical intern. He was really a great sport, while she hammered his joints to test his reflexes, checked his heart, and listened to his lungs. She mimicked everything she had repeatedly experienced the past few months, and it was almost comical. He drew the line when she told him he needed to lie down on the table. She knows the routine. And she refused to get her blood pressure checked. That's our Ashley!

When we asked the neurologist if her recovery process was normal, his reply was, "I don't know, we really never see many cases like this." When we asked if we could expect any long-term issues or concerns, his reply was, "Well of course you should be concerned, but all we can really do is HOPE!"

I wanted to say, WELL, we've already got that covered! How do you think Ashley's standing before you today? Were the tattoos on my foot and Tim's wrist not flashing neon signs for the degree of HOPE and BELIEF we have poured out the past 3 months!

Once again it was a sign to us that there are some things that medical science simply cannot explain. They are called MIRACLES from God! And we should EXPECT them every day!

Quotes of the day:

Once you choose hope, anything's possible.
— Christopher Reeve

Most of the important things in the world have been accomplished by people who have kept on trying when there seemed to be no hope at all.
— Dale Carnegie

Love and Prayers,
Sondra, Tim, Ashley, Nicole

Nicole had grown accustomed to having her big sis back at home. Although Nicole grew up a little bit while Ashley was away for those two months, now there are a few more "turf battles" that occur over which toys belong to whom! Since this whole experience, I have found that when I'm getting upset over two little girls arguing, I stop and think about how there was a time that wasn't even possible. And the childish arguments, while not welcomed, are tolerated a little more than before.

Ashley had become the "social leader" at Madonna Day Rehab. She said hello to everyone. She knew her way around well enough to be a tour guide. She joked and laughed with everyone in the rehab lounge. She played with their walking canes. She touched their body casts. She asked lots and lots of questions. And she told everyone, "I hope you get better soon. I am praying for you!"

The number one question she asked everyone was, "What's your name again?" After about the third or fourth time she asked that question, I'd noticed that pretty consistently, she didn't ask it of the same person anymore. And the reason was simple. She had heard it enough times to click in her memory, and she then began to greet that person by name every time she saw him or her.

Now, think about how many times you've met someone, and seconds after meeting them, you can't remember their name. How horrifying and embarrassing is that? I'll admit it happens to me ALL the time. It feels so silly to say, "What was your name again? I know you just told it to me, but I've already forgotten."

Watching Ashley, I came to realize it's actually normal. It's the natural way that our brains function. When I first heard Ashley constantly asking people's names, I thought to myself, "Poor dear, she doesn't remember them." Then I realized, she did remember them. She was just doing what was necessary to create the imprint in her memory to be able to properly recall the name.

In the beginning, the doctors had warned us that Ashley's personality could be completely different after her brain trauma. Watching her become a little social butterfly with her rehabilitation friends helped me to know that our special little girl was fully returning to us. In fact, I believed that she had even developed a new level of caring and understanding for people who are injured or sick.

♥ ♥ ♥

It was very clear that Ashley was using her special gifts to help and inspire others. She wanted to visit the boy with the football injury, whose family we had visited at the hospital a few weeks earlier. He was now beginning his healing journey at Madonna. Amazingly, he was staying in the same room as Ashley! The Miracle Room!

When we entered the Pediatric/Brain Injury In-patient Area at Madonna, Ashley said, "We are looking for the boy with the football." She was immediately led to his room. She marched in there, hugged the boy's mom, sat down and held his hand. She had no inhibitions and required no encouragement from me. She knew what she was there to do. I saw God's work in Ashley, and it was inspiring!

Thanks Madonna

Amazingly after 6 weeks of in-patient treatment at Madonna Rehabilitation Hospital, and 6 weeks of out-patient Day Rehab at Madonna, we said our goodbyes to the wonderful, caring people there.

Ashley was absolutely beaming with joy and pride today! We took a special cake to Madonna and some little presents for all of Ashley's teachers, nurses, therapists (she loves to give presents)! And most of all lots of hugs and thank yous! We sang a "celebration song" that Grandma Sharon composed! Ashley blushed and giggled, as she was surrounded by all the special people that helped in her healing.

Nicole was right there to cheer her on and have her last moments of fun alongside Ashley in therapy. I wonder if she will ever remember the time she spent at such a young age by her sister's side, being such a huge part of her healing process?

It was interesting to notice today that as many of Ashley's former in-patient nurses and therapists came by to celebrate with us, Ashley did not remember them. She was actually a little shy when they called her by name (or nickname such as chicken-nugget-dude!). It's interesting to now realize that the 6 weeks that were the most critical to her therapy and healing, and probably the most difficult 6 weeks for us, are such a vague memory to Ashley. She really does not remember much of that time.

We visited her old room today to check in on her "football buddy," and once again she did not remember the room! (Of course Nicole did, as she asked to use the bathroom!)

I remember the first night we arrived at Madonna during a tornado warning and everyone was taking shelter. It was such an awkward, scary time. Tim and I both stayed with Ashley those first couple nights. She wasn't talking, walking, eating, and barely stayed awake. We felt like we were in such a foreign place. And leaving there today, it felt totally different … warm, friendly, caring, an atmosphere of healing and hope!

So on the following Monday, Ashley will enter the doors of her elementary school again as a student! She is so excited and hasn't let me forget that we need to go school shopping this weekend. We are talking "power shopping time"! Ashley will start out with half days and will continue to do some out-patient therapy at the pediatric hospital. And we'll gradually adjust the schedule to suit her needs.

The team at school has been wonderful to work with. We have had to make a difficult decision to retain Ashley in first grade rather than moving on to second grade. This may be difficult for her to understand in the beginning. We, in conjunction with her teachers and therapists at Madonna, feel it will be the best approach to position Ashley for continued success. Especially given that there is still a lot of rehabilitation that needs to occur with her right hand and her writing skills.

Love and Prayers,
Sondra, Tim, Ashley, Nicole

I'm not sure if Ashley really understood the magnitude of what we were celebrating—the end of her rehabilitation at Madonna. But she loves cake, so that was a reason for celebration by itself.

Life Lesson: Anything Is Possible

I can honestly say I've witnessed a miracle. There was no surgery or drug that healed my daughter. It was quite simply a tremendous amount of love and positive energy, combined with amazing strength and determination on her part. I hope that she will always remember how incredibly strong she is. I hope that Nicole will always remember how incredibly wonderful and caring she is. And I know for certain that I will never, ever look at any situation again and believe that it's impossible.

I think about the rehabilitation that occurred in the span of sixty-three days. That's two months. That's a summer vacation. During this short window of time, Ashley re-learned everything that it had taken her seven years of learning and growth and development to master. She went from having the abilities of an infant to that of a first grader in sixty-three days. It's really quite incredible when you think about it.

I can no longer look at anything in my life and think "it can't be done." I can't fathom an excuse that would measure up to what we dealt with as a family and what Ashley dealt with as a young girl.

It was not easy. It took hard physical work and determination. It took skilled, caring occupational, physical, vision, and speech therapists. It took personal and family sacrifices. It took focus and determination. It took constant faith and daily prayer. And it took an absolute, non-wavering belief in our hearts that Ashley could heal. It took believing that anything was possible.

Those who hope in the Lord will renew their strength. They will soar on wings like eagles; they will run and not grow weary, they will walk and not be faint.

— Isaiah 40:31

Chapter Thirteen

New Normal

*F*inally, we were rounding the bend to the next turn in the road, the next chapter of the story! We had so much for which to be grateful!

Ashley had her first week back to school. She was so excited to go back and was beaming the first day when she walked in the doors of elementary school. We went school shopping the weekend prior and bought school supplies, clothes, and a snazzy new backpack. The first day Ashley attended school for the morning.

She didn't want to leave when I picked her up. She said, "Mom I want to eat here. Why can't I stay for lunch?"

So the next day she stayed through lunch and recess and then a little longer the following day. She kept telling me she didn't know why she had to leave early. But we wanted to be conservative and not push her too hard.

And, she kept asking, "Mom, why are you driving me to school? I want to ride the bus!" So she began attending full days and riding the bus!

There were signs that Ashley's healing was continuing. Ashley also began therapy assessments at the pediatric hospital. She began by having therapy three days per week. This would be in addition to her therapy she receives in school. Her motor skills continued to improve. And her delightful personality was certainly back.

Her control with her right hand was improving, and slowly her ability to write with her right hand continued to progress. She was beginning to form letters and words and to draw some pictures. It was very encouraging to see the progress she had made compared to several weeks ago when she would not use her right hand at all. She had become aware that she needed to keep using it and practicing for it to get better. She would often say, "Look, Mom, Dad, I used my right hand!"

Ashley worked hard at trying to re-learn to write and draw.

When Ashley had her first spelling test, she was so proud to come home and tell us about it. "Mom, Mom, I have a surprise for you! I got one-hundred percent on my spelling test!" She was grinning from ear to ear.

She always enjoyed spelling, but writing the words was a new challenge for Ashley. Her writing would continue to improve over time.

Ashley's return to first grade seemed to be okay with her. When people asked her what grade she was in, I heard her tell people that she's "going to be in second grade, after she finishes with first grade." It seemed that she was taking it in stride and just having fun being back to school.

Nicole missed Ashley dearly once she was back in school. The girls had spent endless hours together while Ashley was going through rehabilitation. Nicole had been right there by Ashley's side cheering her on constantly. Nicole cried the first day when Ashley's bus left. And all day long kept saying, "Mom, let's just go to Ashley's school and get her!"

Nicole had her first day of preschool, which she began attending two mornings per week. She had a new backpack as well! And she was very proud. She marched right in! The teacher had to remind her to tell Mom goodbye. It was a good thing for her to have her own school and friends on which she could focus. She was proud to have her school artwork displayed in the kitchen now!

Eventually, Tim and I decided to make some significant adjustments to our family. After eighteen years, I decided to resign my corporate sales position to be present at home. We had to say goodbye to our dear friend and nanny, Mica, as her employer. But we knew that she would always have a special place in Ashley and Nicole's lives. They continued to say she's the "best nanny in the world."

I became a full-time mom, shuttling the girls to and from school and Ashley's therapy appointments. Having a career and contributing to the family income had been a significant role for me, so I decided to launch a new global Internet health and wellness business. This was something I could do while I was present with my family. I just couldn't bear the thought of corporate boardrooms and traveling to distant cities, in light of what we had experienced.

I had many hours and late nights staying with Ashley to think about what I really wanted to do. I thought a lot about my career and realized that it was time to shift my priorities. I wanted to do something that I felt had a deep purpose. It was exciting, but it was also a lot of change. We continued to believe that things happen for a reason. And we'd gained a new sense of perspective as a family, so we had decided to carry that with us in how we chose to live our lives.

We knew that our journey would continue, and you never really know what lies ahead. But we now know that our faith and belief could carry us through anything.

We enjoyed creating new memories like visiting the zoo, swimming, celebrating birthdays, and eating out at Mexican restaurants! All the things we loved to do as a family. We just cherished every single moment, because we had discovered what it was like to not have those moments.

One of the best new memories we created was on Halloween. It was the most perfect autumn day in Nebraska that anyone could ask for. Great weather, sunshine, and golden leaves scattered about. And the best part was the smiles and laughter and sounds of "trick-or-treat" throughout the neighborhood.

I now have a quote hanging above the doorway leading from the house to the garage. It's there to remind us whenever we are scrambling to get somewhere on time: "We may not have it all together, but together we have it all!"

One morning, Ashley came into our bedroom at five o'dark-thirty in the morning to tell us that she had lost a tooth! Not only had she lost a tooth, but she had pulled it out on her own. And she was holding that tiny little white baby tooth between her thumb and pointer finger, with the biggest grin I could see at such an early hour.

It occurred to me later that the tooth that finally had come out was loose back when Ashley was at the pediatric hospital. In fact, after she came out of the comatose state, one of the immediate reactions from her nervous system was severe teeth grinding. At this moment, as I looked back and thought about it, I remembered "trying" to sleep in her hospital room amidst the teeth grinding that seemed to go on all night. It had gotten so severe that we had asked that a dentist come in to look at fitting her with a tooth guard.

One of the concerns at that time was this one little loose tooth! Would all the grinding cause it to fall out and be a choking concern? There was a suggestion offered to "pull it out!" We just couldn't bear the thought of another procedure with anesthesia, so we chose not to pursue that route. Eventually the grinding subsided.

Amazingly, I had forgotten all about the loose tooth. It seemed so ironic that after all of that, Ashley, the strong, courageous girl, pulled the tooth out on her own, in the middle of the night without swallowing or dropping the darn little thing and proudly marched into our room to announce that the extraction was complete.

That night we proceeded with the ritual of placing the tooth in a little purple bag and tucking it under her pillow. The next morning, when she lifted her pillow to find three dollars, she was so happy. She was running around saying, "Mom, Mom, it's an exciting day. The tooth fairy came and gave me three dollars!" We immediately had to pull out the pink piggy bank and tuck the dollars in his belly! And then Nicole began asking if her teeth would soon fall out so she could get money from the tooth fairy!

♥ ♥ ♥

During this season of our lives, we discovered the people in our lives who were the most important. It was the people who came to our side and stuck with us through the most challenging moments. My mom was one of the people who stayed strong like a ROCK through our journey with Ashley. She really has been right there by our side since the moment Ashley was born and diagnosed with congenital heart disease. She held our hand through Ashley's first heart surgery at three months of age. She was by our side during the first two and a half months Ashley spent in the hospital as an infant.

After Ashley's first heart surgery, she had to have a tracheotomy. Her airways were not strong enough to hold up without breathing support. So for the first five months after her heart operation, she had the help of a bi-pap breathing machine. Ashley had her trach for a year and a half. My mom, Sharon, took the training right alongside Tim and me to learn how to suction and change the trach. We are not talking about a grandma who just changes diapers. This is a lady who learned the skills of trained medical professionals to be able to take care of her precious grandbaby.

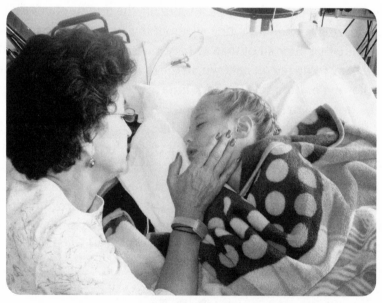

Grandma Sharon and Ashley. I love this picture because it shows the depth of love and concern my mother has for Ashley.

And once again, my mom had been right by our side with Ashley and Nicole as we embarked on the incredibly challenging journey of Ashley's healing after the stroke. It's no wonder that Ashley and Grandma Sharon have such an incredibly special bond. Ashley's ritual is to call Grandma Sharon every day. My mom is an incredibly special, strong, amazing lady! We are so fortunate to have her by our sides, always willing to drive long distances and make personal sacrifices for the sake of her grandchildren. That is pure gold love.

We had been truly blessed for the wonderful family and friends in our lives. When we celebrated our first Thanksgiving after Ashley's stroke, we talked about what Thanksgiving means. Ashley said it's about being grateful for family and taking care of each other. And isn't that the truth!

We enjoyed our first post-stroke Thanksgiving feast at the lodge at a local state park and then we told the girls we would go hiking in the woods. They were so excited. Most importantly, we were happy to be together. It was amazing to see Ashley and Nicole hiking and being active outside.

We were truly, truly blessed to have traveled this journey together. In honor of Thanksgiving Day, here is our unique family meal prayer:

For this time together,
For this food we share,
For this LOVE we feel,
Father in Heaven,
We Thank You.

♥ ♥ ♥

A couple days after Ashley's surgery at a very difficult moment in time, a special friend told us a story of hope. It was something we could look forward to doing as a family. She was going to nominate Ashley for a wish with the Make-A-Wish Foundation. Her message was clear that we would get through this. And Ashley would be all right.

Many months later, we realized that dream come true. Ashley was honored by the Make-A-Wish Foundation. Our family experienced an unbelievable fairytale trip to Disney World in Florida. The girls were showered with gifts including princess dolls and magic wands, games, books, beach towels, swimsuits, PJ's, and more. Everything required for a fairytale vacation! Nicole loved the talking mirror that says, "Your hair looks like a princess!"

A limousine took us to the airport the day of the trip. And we stayed at a special resort called "Give Kids the World." There was a twenty-four-hour ice cream parlor and many other wonderful kids' attractions. We had the opportunity to visit the Disney Theme Parks, SeaWorld, Animal Kingdom, and, at Ashley's request, go to the BEACH!

Ashley was treated like a princess during the week we spent at Disney in Orlando thanks to Make-A-Wish.

Due to the generous contributions by so many people, we had the privilege to go on this amazing adventure. After the difficult journey we had traveled the previous summer, I was confident that this was God's way of rewarding us for our endurance and faith. It was His way of erasing the pain and sad memories and replacing them with happy ones.

"Celebrate Everyday"—the signs in front of the Disney Animal Kingdom read! We celebrated in the most amazing way. Ashley turned to me at one point and said, "Isn't this just amazing?" Yes, it was amazing!

And during the Lion King performance, Ashley thanked me for getting the BELIEVE tattoo to help her get better! My response, "I would do ANYTHING for you!" On this day, it was apparent to me that Ashley was beginning to put it all together and truly understood that the trip to Disney was a celebration of joy for her strength and perseverance.

Ashley got her biggest wish of all. She made it back to the beach.

Life Lesson: Pay Attention to the Signs

I believe that each of us has a predetermined plan for our lives. This goes back to my point that we are not in control. We believe we are. And so we spend much of our energy trying to resist the natural course our lives are supposed to take. When we are in a place of full transparency and awareness, there are signs guiding us.

Before Ashley's stroke, I can honestly say I was missing all the signs. I was headstrong in believing that I knew what was best. I have been known to say that missing the subtle signs led God to dig out a two-by-four board and slam it over my head! Honestly, that's the most vivid analogy I can offer to describe the depth of pain we felt during Ashley's stroke. Only then was I shaken enough to realize that I needed to chart a new course.

“ **You made all the delicate, inner parts of my body and knit me together in my mother's womb. Thank You for making me so wonderfully complex! Your workmanship is marvelous— and how well I know it.** ”

— Psalm 139:13-14

Chapter Fourteen

What It's Like to Be a Heart Hero

*S*everal months after Ashley's stroke, I was working on a video slide show, a visual journal of Ashley's recovery process. Ashley awoke from a nap, and when she peered over my shoulder and looked at some of the pictures, she became upset and very, very emotional. I realized how scary some of her memories of that summer must be for a young child.

Even though I suspect there is a lot she does not remember, I can only imagine that what she remembers—combined with the bits and pieces we have told her, and the unrecognizable pictures of herself—was frightening. I hope that this book and the journal and pictures we have kept, while difficult for her to understand right now, will be helpful to her someday when she is older and has a need to understand the miracle that she is.

For a child with a congenital heart defect, regular cardiology checkups are "routine." However, I had learned to never underestimate anything that is labeled routine where Ashley's health is concerned. So it goes that I might just be stricken with panic the morning of a scheduled doctor's visit. When that happens, I know that I can call a fellow heart mom or turn to the online journal and put out a request for prayers. At the press of a button, hundreds of prayers are in the works! And I believe there is power in prayer. And you never know when you need to call on that power.

Ashley had her first cardiology checkup after the stroke, and she was asking a lot of questions. "Will I get a poke? Will I have to take my shirt off? Will they use that jelly on my heart?"

The funniest question of all was, "Mom, why don't they use peanut butter on my heart instead of jelly?" I cracked up! You see, Ashley does not like jelly. But she LOVES peanut butter!

We went together as a family to give Ashley encouragement. The girls and I met Tim for pizza before the appointment to make it feel like a special day. It's these kinds of little strategies that we've learned to use to make these visits less scary for her—and for all of us.

Ashley was very brave, and she even allowed for three blood pressure checks. Even these simple blood pressure checks bring on significant anxiety. Then, she lay on the table and watched a movie and was really a big girl for the heart echo. She even looked at the screen and asked if that was her heart! She was very proud to take home a picture of her heart and asked if she could take it to school to show her friends.

Her cardiologist had very good results to share and said the valve is functioning well and we should come back for a checkup in a year! WOW! A whole year! You see, Ashley's valve will not grow with her. She will eventually need surgery again to replace it. The life expectancy of the valve is five to ten years, and we are hopeful that her next valve replacement can be done via heart catheterization rather than open-heart surgery.

At that moment, we were happy to have a year ahead of us to enjoy being heart healthy. Ashley's cardiologist was also very happy to see the amazing progress she has made in the recovery from her brain injury, since he last saw her when she was still hospitalized. The medical students with him were impressed as well. Ashley was able to show her entourage of curious medical team members what a miracle looks like.

♥ ♥ ♥

When life is good, we sometimes let our guard down. It's easy to slip into a comfort zone and begin to take some things for granted. I never want to "jinx" things! Yet sometimes we still get a gentle "nudge" from God to remind us how precious life is.

I remember a lesson in belief that I got straight from Ashley.

I was reading the girls books at bedtime. They each picked a book. Nicole picked *The Fairy Princess,* of course! Ashley picked *The Children's Dictionary.*

I said, "Okay, we'll read one item."

For whatever reason, Ashley said, "Mom, read about pumpkins."

So I flipped to the word *pumpkin,* and she proceeded to tell me that I wasn't on the right page. I showed her the word *pumpkin* and read the description.

She persisted. "No, Mom, there's a different page with a picture of a pumpkin." I flipped the pages. No picture.

Ashley said, "MOM, YOU GOTTA BELIEVE ME. There's a picture of a pumpkin in this book."

I said, "Okay, perhaps it is under a different word."

I tried *Jack-o-lantern, Halloween, vegetable,* and several others and pleaded with her that it must have been a different book.

She persisted, "MOM, YOU GOTTA BELIEVE ME. There's a picture of a pumpkin in this book."

In fact, she said it's big and it's lying on its side. I grabbed another book and flipped to the word *pumpkin.* No picture.

I said, "Ashley, I don't know what to tell you. It MUST be in another book that you saw this picture of a pumpkin!"

And again she said, "MOM, YOU GOTTA BELIEVE ME. There's a picture of a pumpkin in this book."

I was intrigued to find out if there really was, so I began flipping through every page, while Nicole is rubbing her eyes, ready to go to sleep. FINALLY! The picture of the pumpkin! Under the word *HUGE*—a picture of a huge pumpkin.

If you could have seen Ashley's face, it was priceless! Her big brown eyes staring at me, and then this little grin, "MOM, I TOLD YOU IT WAS IN THIS BOOK!"

" Mom, You Gotta Believe Me! "

— Ashley Dubas

♥ ♥ ♥

Have you ever been afraid to do something? Yet no matter how scared you were, you had to do it anyway? That was Ashley with her first EEG (brain scan)! She was very brave and did a great job. However, it took a lot of coaxing, reassurance, and patience.

You see, Ashley doesn't remember that she's previously had EEG tests. She was not conscious when she had the last round of EEG tests in the summer of 2008. So this was something new for her and she did not know what to expect. Considering the latest MRI test that was rather traumatic, she was not too willing to trust us when we told her that there would not be any "owies" or "pokes."

After considerable stalling, picking out a movie, not wanting to lie down, and then needing to use the restroom, I took Ashley aside. I took her face in my hands and looked her in the eyes. I said to her, "I promise you no one is going to poke or hurt you today, and if they try we will go home. It is important to have this test so the doctor can understand how we can help you. Let's get this over with so we can go have ice cream." We laid our hands one on top of the other like a sports team does and said, "Let's do it!"

Ashley and I lay down together and watched Dora and Diego, while the twenty-three probes were "glued" to her head. Tim held the portable DVD player for us. Ashley was not happy with the gauze bandage they wrapped around her head to keep the probes in place. But she stayed tough, as her chin quivered and a few tears rolled out of her eye. Once the probes were on, the actual test only took about fifteen minutes. The lights were turned off, and I snuggled up to Ashley and actually fell asleep—tired from keeping her up late the night before!

I was so proud of Ashley! She is very strong. Sometimes stronger than I am, I think! We picked up Nicole and went out for dinner as a family ... and got ice cream.

We are all familiar with the no-news-is-good-news expression. Is it always true? I like to think there are answers to everything. But what if there are not? Ashley and Nicole ask hundreds of questions all day long. And I have to admit sometimes I'm really stumped. Sometimes I just don't have the answers.

I have come to learn that having exact answers as it relates to Ashley's health, and in particular her neurological health, is not always possible. Sometimes I've been in a quandary about whether to pursue more information and answers. Or whether to accept what we know and let it go. One thing I know after all that we've been through with Ashley, as a family, is that sometimes it is really nice to just enjoy "normal" when things are normal. And I want to resist thinking now is anything other than that. There's also the fear of what's ahead. There will be more surgeries, cardiology visits, MRIs, EEGs, and medical tests. In fact our lifetime, and Ashley's, will be full of them! So I really don't want to conjure up beliefs that anything is wrong if it's not.

One thing I have learned for sure, however, is to trust my gut. I even find for myself that routine events like this trigger emotions and memories of our past time spent in the hospital. And it is difficult. The anxiety is there for Tim and me too.

Coping Strategies: Realize that Nothing Is Routine

Often times, medical professionals will use the word routine. They will say things like, "This is a routine procedure, test, or surgery." Ashley's surgery was supposed to be "routine." We created an expectation that is what would happen.

I'm certainly not suggesting that you should operate with less than positive expectations; however, I think that you must operate in a mode of "awareness" when dealing with any tragic situation. The "things that rarely happen" do at some point happen.

Ask questions. Don't be ashamed that you don't know the medical terminology. It's your right as a patient or family member to have information explained in a way that you understand. It's what you need to do in order to make empowered decisions and be a good advocate for yourself or your loved one. Understand the risks and make decisions based on a full understanding. Ask for help from a friend who may have experience with a situation or condition.

Trust your intuition. And then trust in the professionals and exercise your faith.

> **I am beginning to learn that it is the sweet, simple things of life which are the real ones after all.**
>
> — Laura Ingalls Wilder

Chapter Fifteen

Choices

*H*aving choices in how we choose to live our lives is something I came to really appreciate during that year. I always offer the girls "choices." Sometimes, the options may include "going to timeout." And sometimes I am shocked when they choose timeout over what they've been asked to do! Ashley and Nicole are both strong-willed little girls. They take after their mom. I do believe it is important for them to always appreciate that they have options in life.

As a family, we were faced with some challenging choices during that year. As parents, Tim and I were faced with the difficult decision to have Ashley's heart valve replaced. Although it was not really a choice, as we always knew the day would come. We will be faced with similar choices in the future.

We did not have a choice in the initial trauma that Ashley experienced that summer during her surgery. However, we made the choice to BELIEVE that Ashley would pull through and fully recover. We made the choice to see all that was possible. We made the choice to focus on our family and rethink our priorities in life. One of the outcomes was my resignation from the corporate world and launch of a new business—a decision we've never regretted as it has brought us closer together.

We made a choice to have Ashley re-enter school at the first-grade level, not where she would have been, in second grade. This is a decision, despite our initial concerns, that turned out to be a great choice for Ashley. The teachers, principal, therapists, and everyone at school did an amazing job at helping Ashley in her re-entry to school, two months later than her classmates and a grade lower. She made new friends and bee-bopped to the school bus every day with delight. This enabled her to be better positioned to tackle new learning in second grade the following year.

In an effort to keep life more simple, we made a choice to sell our house and move to a new, smaller house. This was initially a difficult decision for us to leave our home of eight years. We had so many memories in that house. Ashley was only ten days old when we moved in. And Nicole was born while we lived here. So much happened there. Nonetheless, we knew that the love of a family is what makes a house a home, not bricks and walls. Moving to a smaller home would mean that I could continue to work from home and be more present for Ashley and Nicole.

Ashley's journey has taught us the value of having choices. We have said that we believe that her journey happened for a reason. IT HAPPENED FOR A REASON!

To be able to focus more energy on being present in our girls' lives, we are following through on our commitment that I am home with the girls, and to simplify our lives! I'll continue to work on growing our health and wellness business, while working around our family's schedule. And in an uncertain economy, selling our house was the right decision: less pressure, less stress, more time to enjoy life! The girls actually were really excited about the move. They have enjoyed having Mom at home and saw the move as an adventure. Not for a second have I doubted or second-guessed the decisions of that year. We continue to have gratitude each day for the blessings we have.

A very good friend gave me a key chain a couple years ago that says, "Live the Life You Love." When you turn it over it says,

"Love the Life You Live." When she gave it to me, I remember "wishfully thinking" that would be nice. Now I realize that we just have to make it so. And remember that our children are watching and learning from us. And let them teach us in return ... to live life!

Now I can honestly say that this experience has taught me that we have choices in life. We always have choices. We can choose what we do for work, where we live, who we spend time with, and how we think about what's happening in our life. Choosing to be happy in the face of adversity has become a way of life. My new motto for life became: "Success is living your life the way you choose."

Life Lesson: You Have Choices about How to Live Your Life

Success can mean a lot of different things to different people. I used to think success was about career and the size of your bank account. And I felt trapped by the success I had realized. Other people may feel they have no choices in life. They may feel they are destined to have a life of challenge and hardship.

I discovered that we truly are limited more by our minds than our circumstances. There were circumstances throughout our daughter's healing journey that seemed unimaginable. We chose to deal with the situation in a way that was positive. We chose to learn from the experience instead of being bitter and resentful. We chose to let go of the past and redesign our future.

"When one door of happiness closes, another opens; but often we look so long at the closed door that we do not see the one which has opened for us. "

— Helen Keller

Chapter Sixteen

Letting Go

A year had come and gone since Ashley's stroke. Ashley celebrated her eighth birthday hula-hooping and eating cake and ice cream, with chocolate from ear to ear! She had a couple close friends over for a party, and they did water slides and ran through the sprinkler.

Ashley drew a picture the other day and on it she wrote: "I was seven, and now I am eight!" Simple and true! It was a symbol to me to just keep things simple. Life is easier that way.

Remember how I kept Ashley's pajamas in my bag and wouldn't wash them until she came home from Madonna. Well, I have another secret to share. This is something even Tim didn't know at the time. I have a voice message on my cell phone of Ashley's voice from Wednesday, June 4, 2008, a few weeks prior to her surgery. I had been on a business trip and she had left me a voicemail to let me know that a friend she had invited would not be able to come to her birthday party.

I was haunted by that message when I discovered it on my phone while Ashley was comatose. Then it became my source of daily strength, to hear her voice and believe that she would come back to us. Tim listened to the message with me that day in the hospital, but he had no idea that I had been keeping it all this time. I had another voicemail that I had not deleted. It was a voicemail of the first word Ashley spoke when she was recovering last summer, *Icky*. She kept saying *icky* over and over and over again. My mom was at Madonna with Ashley and called so that we could hear Ashley's voice, which, at that time, we had not heard for over five weeks.

Why had I kept these messages on my phone for a year? I wasn't really sure. I just knew that it didn't feel right to delete them. Whenever I would hear them, it would be a reminder to me to cherish my children.

The third message on my phone was Nicole's sweet little voice saying, "Mommy, blankie." I had forgotten and taken her blankie with me in the car one day on my way home from therapy. And so keeping Nicole's message was another "safety net." The what-if feeling that if something would happen to her, I would want to be able to hear that message. I have to confess that four years later I still practice this ritual of saving messages on my phone from my children, "just in case."

We were learning to "let go" of a lot of things. Some of them were thoughts and emotions. And others were truly "things." We had made our decision to simplify our lives and spend more time together as a family, without me working full-time. And so we prepared to hand over the keys of our home of eight years to proud new owners.

On that same day, I deleted the voicemail messages and decided it was time to move on. It was time for our family to focus on the future. It was going to be a new start for us. So we cleared the last of our possessions from our house, packed our bags, and headed for Estes Park, Colorado, which was one of our favorite family vacation spots.

A week of relaxation and fresh mountain air! It was another chance to create new memories and buffer some of the sadness of leaving our old house. Estes Park is a peaceful, tranquil place. I think of it as a "healing" place. We stayed at a little riverside inn and roasted marshmallows by the fire every night. I celebrated my birthday while we were there. The entire day, Ashley told every single person we met, "It's my mom's birthday today! She's forty-one!"

The previous year was the big forty milestone, which came and went without fanfare while Ashley was at Madonna. This year I had the most amazing birthday with Tim, my mom, and the girls! It was absolutely the best day ever with all my favorite people and things to do: Starbucks, spa, shopping, and dinner and wine with my family in the mountains.

Ashley hiked 2.2 miles in the Rocky Mountains. She led the way and was amazingly resilient! Poor little Nicole had sore feet and coaxed Grandma Sharon into carrying her piggy-back all the way back down. It was a beautiful day and a wonderful trip.

The best birthday ever because our family was together—happy and healthy in one of my favorite places in the mountains. Peace had returned to our lives.

It was a major transition moving to a new home. We packed for a month and then had no home to call our own for almost a month. It was a truly humbling experience. Thank goodness we had kind, generous, patient friends who took us in.

Once we were moved into our new house and settled, we loved it! It felt like home. There was a forest in our backyard with a hundred-year-old tree! And we could sit in the backyard and roast marshmallows by the fire pit. If I closed my eyes and listened to the wind blow in the trees, I could almost imagine we were back at our favorite little mountain-side retreat.

Our goal with this transition was to simplify our lives and focus on our family. Tim and I both felt a great sense of accomplishment in doing that. However, I'm not going to lie. There was still a lot of emotion attached to the way our life used to be and the significance we had placed on things like our big, beautiful house.

I believe in "signs" that guide us and remind us we are on the right path. Twice within a week of our move, in two different states, I saw two different billboard signs that read: "The Most Important Things in Life are Not Things." These billboards were not advertising anything in particular. They were just simple statements.

I remember feeling a chill all over my body when I saw the first sign. And then I nodded to myself, as if knowing this was my "sign" that we were making the right choices. When I saw the second sign, my mouth dropped open! This was not a coincidence. It was a very clear message to reinforce our decision, just in case there was any lingering doubt. The signs don't get clearer than that.

I have often said that our experience with Ashley's stroke was like a two-by-four board hitting me over the head. I believe that sometimes when you miss the small signs that are there to guide you on your path, God takes drastic measures to ensure that you find your way to the path He has designed for you. And that's exactly how I have come to view this experience.

Life Lesson: Sometimes You've Got to Make Changes

Change is not easy. It's normal to experience grief, anxiety, and doubt. However, when you can experience change from the standpoint of growth and opportunity for expansion, it makes it easier. Quitting a high-paying job, staying home with my kids, starting a new business, and selling our home were not easy choices. They were changes that we had the "opportunity" to make because we could now see a different kind of future.

It's been said that the definition of insanity is doing the same thing and expecting a different result. As I look back on our experience, I realize that we were forced by circumstance to make some of the changes we did. Our daughter needed a level of care and support that was no longer practical for us to manage with my travel schedule. And, quite simply, I realized I didn't want to do it anymore.

There was a very profound "aha" moment for me that I'll never forget. It was a beautiful summer day. I was working in my home office while Tim had taken Ashley to her daily rehabilitation. Our nanny was outside playing sidewalk chalk with Nicole and the neighbor kids. And I was grueling over a hundred-page contract.

It was like an out-of-body experience. I couldn't figure out why I was having such a difficult time concentrating on the work that had become so natural to me. I suddenly became aware that I was forcing myself to do something that I no longer had a passion for doing. The light bulb turned on in my head. And I knew the time had come for a change. Once I allowed myself to accept that reality, there was no turning back. And it was incredibly "freeing."

Life Lesson: Put Your Priorities into Perspective

As I mentioned earlier, money doesn't buy happiness. Time is a precious gift and how we choose to spend our time is never more important than when you are faced with the prospect of losing time with your loved ones. The endless hours of solitude and waiting forced me to really think about what was important to me. It was a significant soul-searching experience. It was a forced reality check.

We had become more "grounded" in what was important to us individually and as married couple, and as a family. The transitions we made as a family as a result were not easy. Selling our dream house and giving up my corporate salary were not easy. However, it no longer mattered "what other people thought." It only mattered what we felt was right for us.

We decided to live our lives according to our own standards. For us that meant simplicity and time together. I felt a "transparency" and sense of freedom that I had never felt before.

Ashley Today

At the time of publishing, Ashley has been "heart healthy" now for over four years. She visits her cardiologist annually. Our hope is that her current heart valve will last for at least ten years. And she should be a candidate by then for a replacement that is done via catheterization instead of the invasive open-heart procedure. We will hope and pray for that to be the case.

She has had some relapses, neurologically, with some seizure-type episodes. The neurologists believe that she will always be prone to seizures due to the brain damage that exists. Ashley participates in a specialized learning program at school. Her handwriting has improved immensely. She's learned to use both hands by writing with her right hand and eating with her left hand. She says her right hand causes her to miss her mouth.

She has very few apparent side effects from her surgery and brain injury. And she is certainly a special little child—always so happy and loving! We continue to believe that God has great plans for her.

Ashley has very limited memory of her rehabilitation. I hope that this book will help her to one day understand the magnitude of what she experienced and the impact she has had on so many people. Most importantly, I want her to know how deeply she is loved.

"Children hold our hands for a moment but our hearts forever. ""

— Anonymous

About Heart Heroes, Inc.

*L*ike Ashley, more than 40,000 babies are born each year with congenital heart defects (CHD). That's about 1 out of every 100 babies born. CHD is the number-one birth-defect-related cause of death. Scientists do not yet know what causes hearts to develop abnormally, but advancements in the techniques to repair little hearts occur every year.

For kids undergoing heart procedures, being alone without their family to comfort them amidst a crowd of medical professionals is absolutely frightening. Heart Hero capes were created with the hope that all children visiting the hospital for surgery or their cardiologist will feel invincible wearing their capes. Their cape will give them superhero powers to cope with their challenges. And their parents will be comforted knowing that the arms that always protect them are momentarily being substituted with the super powers of the cape.

Kitty Burton and I were brought together by fate during Ashley's recovery. We were two women who did not know each other previously, but shared a common bond. That common bond was our children with congenital heart defects and the challenges our families face daily in dealing with our child's condition.

After seeing our children face the challenges of heart operations and cardiology appointments, together in 2009, we created Heart

Heroes, Inc.. Since then, Heart Hero capes have been mailed to children in nine different countries and forty-five states.

A portion of proceeds from this book will be donated to Heart Heroes, Inc., so that Heart Heroes around the world can experience their life-saving power!

If you know a child with CHD who wishes to have a cape or you would like to make a donation, visit the Heart Heroes website at www.heartherocapes.com. Join our Facebook Group: Heart Heroes, and follow us on Twitter: @HeartHeroes.

"Super Sam" is Ashley's fellow Heart Hero and son of Heart Heroes co-founder Kitty Burton. Ashley and Sam share a special bond.

Ashley models her Heart Hero cape a few years after her stroke.

Everything we do should be a result of our gratitude for what God has done for us.

— Lauryn Hill

Special Tributes

I feel tremendous gratitude for the outcome of this experience for our family. Words cannot express our sincere, deep appreciation to so many people who offered support and encouragement during our journey. I realize that I could never properly thank everyone, so this is my tribute to all of you and our attempt to extend our gratitude to everyone.

During Ashley's recovery—

Thanks, first of all to God for working a miracle for Ashley, for giving us our family back. For showing us there is a better life to be had, and showing us what belief, hope, and love can produce ... joy!

Thank you for the abundance of prayers! And the many prayer chains!

Thank you for the hugs when we needed them the most.

Thank you to my mom for everything, for being by our sides and Ashley's. You are the kind of mother I aspire to be.

Thank you to my brother, Mike, and Rochelle. You didn't leave our side that entire first week. Having you with us and Ashley meant the world!

Thank you to my dad, Larry, and his wife, Sunny, for the support and many, many visits.

Thank you and thank you again to Mica, nanny for Ashley and Nicole. We know this was just as hard for you as it was for us. You were their other mommy for five years. You kept the household together and looked after Nicole when we couldn't be there! You're amazing! We love you!

Thank you to Matt, Margaret, Sydney, and Ciera! You are our extended family. Your support has been incredible through this experience and our journey through many life changes. We couldn't ask for better friends.

Thank you to our many wonderful friends who called, texted, emailed, traveled from far places to laugh, cry, and pray with us. As I have said before, friends are like stars. You may not always see them, but you know they are always there.

Thank you to Aunt Mary for the sleepovers with Ashley to give us a break and for being part of the healing process and therapy. Your willingness to leave your family and job to help us was amazing. It gave us the breaks in the sixty-three-day journey that we needed.

Thank you to all of Tim's family for the many trips to visit and being there, especially during those early critical hours when the "emotions" were running a little wild!

Thank you, Grandma Marge, for the continuous supply of homemade "crispies." It was one of the first things Ashley ate once she could. And to Aunt Patty for "delivering" them!

Thank you to the pastors from Church of the Master for the continuous visits to the pediatric hospital and Madonna. It was always refreshing to see you and to know that you were praying with us for Ashley.

Thank you to our neighborhood friends for cheering Ashley on. For mowing our lawn all summer. We appreciated the banners and posters and hugs and smiles.

Thank you to the many people who brought hot meals and lunches to the hospital, fruit baskets, and other items we needed.

Thank you to the incredible surgeons, specialists, nurses, and medical staff at the pediatric hospital. We never doubted that Ashley was getting the best possible care.

Thank you to Ashley's surgeon for the amazing work you do and for fixing Ashley's heart a second time. We know there will be more surgeries for Ashley, and we can only hope we will be blessed with having you there with us again.

Thank you to the amazing therapists, nurses, and doctors at Madonna. From the moment we walked in the doors, there was never a doubt from anyone that Ashley would make less than a full recovery. The hard work and determination have paid off.

Thank you to everyone for the wonderful gifts for Ashley and our family. There is hardly a room that you enter in our house that doesn't have some inspirational message somewhere within it that involves the word *BELIEVE*! It is a daily reminder of the blessings we have experienced and what faith and belief can produce.

Speaking of which, how can I forget the BELIEVE tattoo team. It's permanent. That deserves a big thank you. I'm just glad my mom didn't get hers on her forehead. She said she would if it would make a difference.

Thank you to the hundreds of people who followed Ashley's story via the online journal. And to the many people we did not know, until now, who have shown kindness and support. There really is a lot of kindness and compassion in people. (It's hard for me to tell Ashley to be wary of strangers because we've been blessed by some pretty nice "strangers"!)

Thank you to our employers, bosses, and colleagues for supporting us and graciously giving us the time that we needed to mend our family. It is truly wonderful to work for companies that value family and demonstrate it.

Thank you all for continuing to take interest in sharing our journey. It's an honor to be able to share with everyone the power that this little girl has had in influencing our lives. I am reminded that she is our shining light, leading us down the path that God intends for us.

From the bottom of our hearts, thank you. We are truly blessed.

" Of all the attitudes we can acquire, surely the attitude
of gratitude is the most important, and by far the
most life-changing. "

— Zig Ziglar

And in the writing of this book—

Thank you to my dear friend and fellow heart mom Kitty for your belief in me and encouragement. God brought us to each other so that we can do amazing things!

Thank you to my husband for having the patience to let me rediscover myself and for supporting me in life and my work and for understanding why I needed to tell our story.

Thank you to the many friends and family that encouraged me to "tell our story."

Thank you to all the other families of Heart Heroes like Ashley who have continued to inspire me. As I have followed many of your stories, I have known in my heart that we share a special bond, a common understanding about the love for a child that is dealing with a unique medical condition. It is my hope that others will find hope and healing in reading our story.

About the Author

Sondra Dubas is mother of two special young girls and is married to her high school sweetheart. She is a passionate woman who cares about helping others transform their lives, live to their full potential, and cope with adversity. Her family is a central theme in her life. She is a successful business woman and entrepreneur.

Sondra is the owner and founder of Miracle Heart Books, LLC, an independent publishing company that disseminates books that contribute to the healing of children and families that have been affected by congenital heart defects and stroke or brain trauma. Sondra is also co-founder of Heart Heroes, Inc., a nonprofit organization that sends superhero capes to children born with heart defects. Children in nine countries and forty-five states have been touched by this organization.